THE WORLD OF ENGLISH: DRAMA

BEYOND THE FOOTLIGHTS

One-Act Plays for Secondary Schools

selected and edited by

HUGH D. McKELLAR, B.A.

EDWARD ARNOLD

© MACMILLAN COMPANY OF CANADA 1964

First published in this edition 1964
by Edward Arnold (Publishers) Ltd.
41 *Bedford Square, London WC1B 3DP*
Reprinted 1966, 1969, 1971, 1973, 1975, 1976, 1978

ISBN: 0 7131 1243 3

PRINTED IN GREAT BRITAIN BY
WHITSTABLE LITHO LTD, WHITSTABLE, KENT

We gratefully acknowledge the co-operation of Mr. Maurice Hatton in providing the cover photograph

CONTENTS

INTRODUCTION

Originally selected for study and acting by Canadian students in their first two years of secondary school, these seven plays include scripts written for stage, for radio, and for television by authors from six different lands. Most of the authors have also won fame as novelists and poets. While any person who reads one of these plays, or sees it performed, can reasonably expect from it half an hour's enjoyment, he will probably enjoy the play still more if he appreciates the skill with which the author has constructed it.

At first glance it may well appear that the author has simply recorded the details of an interesting half-hour in the lives of three or four people; indeed, this is the impression which a good playwright strives to create. But a little thought will show that the writing of a play is by no means as effortless as this. We who read it are in somewhat the position of dinner guests who arrive to find the house in order and the meal nearly ready to serve; though the hostess and her family may have worked hard all afternoon to achieve this, we see only the end result of their labours. Similarly, behind the smooth surface of a play lies the author's struggle with several difficult problems.

First, he must present to us several CHARACTERS in such a way that we quickly become interested in what happens to them. From their appearance, surroundings, speeches, and actions, we deduce what sort of people they are, and what is the state of their affairs at the moment. As soon as their SITUATION is established, we see the raw materials for CONFLICT: usually one character wants to accomplish something, but is prevented from doing so by another character, by circumstances, or even by his own thoughts and attitudes. Soon matters reach a CRISIS – a point where the main character cannot avoid making a decision about his course of conduct, and we wait with SUSPENSE to see which of the alternatives open to him he will actually choose. No matter what his decision, it brings upon him consequences – and the road is paved for the next crisis. This chain of events, in which each incident is the cause of the next, is the PLOT. The plot reaches its end, and the suspense its highest peak, just before the final crisis or CLIMAX, in which the main conflict of the play is settled.

Basically, the playwright gives us pleasure by first arousing and then satisfying our curiosity about a situation; but often he will further delight us by his skill with language in writing memorable phrases or passages, or by portraying a character so vividly that we feel we know him personally. And a fine artist is likely to build his play around a basic idea or THEME which will continue to intrigue us long after we have closed the book or left the theatre.

Protest, for example, may leave us wondering why the Grandmother really needed to carry her loyalty to tradition to such an extreme; had we been in her place, would we have acted differently? *The Ring of General Macías* may present us with a similar question about Raquel and her devotion to 'honour'. Impressive as these women's behaviour seems in a play, how would they fare in real life with such ideas?

At this point we shall realize that a play is not, and cannot be, a mere transcript of a real-life situation. By carefully *selecting* and *arranging* details, the playwright has imposed a pattern on actual experience. He cannot afford, for instance, to include even one speech which does not contribute something to the progress of the play, whereas in real life people frequently utter words with no discernible purpose in mind. Again, he lets us see only that side of his characters which he wants us to see, with the result that we can judge a person after watching him for a few minutes; real human beings are far too complex to permit such swift judgments to be accurate.

It is precisely because drama – and, for that matter, other forms of literature – can offer us a somewhat simplified but still recognizable version of real life, that plays have been on European school curricula for the last 2,000 years and more. When so much of our happiness and success in life depends on our accurate judgment of people and their actions, we do well to practise on the characters and events of a drama.

We gain even more valuable training for real life when we take part in acting out a good play. If the play is presented on a stage before an audience, we gain such incidental benefits as improvement in our ways of speaking and moving; but even reading the parts at the front of the classroom gives us a fine opportunity to practise putting ourselves in the position of another person. Suppose you are asked to take the part of Timothy in *The Three Wayfarers*. It is unlikely that you have ever been in a gaol cell under sentence of death, and you may not normally have so much nerve and presence of mind as Timothy displays. No matter: somehow you must convey to your listeners the impression that the person before them is not you, but Timothy. You must decide how he would move, how he would speak, how he would approach people; in short, you must gain some insight into Timothy as a person. And the ability to understand another person, whether or not you admire him, is a rare and valuable one in real life.

Your study of drama, then, can become as rewarding for you as you will allow it to be.

REMEMBER CAESAR

by

GORDON DAVIOT

CHARACTERS

Richard, Lord Weston, a judge
Lady Weston, his wife
Mr. Roger Chetwynd, his clerk

PERIOD: Reign of Charles II, 1660–85

A room in the house of RICHARD, LORD WESTON, *on a spring morning in the reign of Charles II. Lord Weston (until his late elevation to the bench, Sir Richard) is not wealthy, and the room is a combination of study and withdrawing-room. Up right is the door to the landing (it is a first-floor room), in the rear wall a large casement window looking out to the front of the house, in the left wall the fireplace, and down from it another window through which one can see the trees in the garden. Up stage of the fireplace a cupboard in the wall. Hanging on the walls and over the fireplace are family portraits.*

LORD WESTON *is seated by the fireplace, a table of books and papers beside him. He is engaged in filling his pipe. And talking.*

Down right, where the light from the side-window falls across his small writing-table, is seated MR. ROGER CHETWYND, *a thin, earnest, absent-minded, and conscientious youth. So conscientious is he that his mind, even when absent, is absent on his employer's business. He has begun by listening to his master's lecture, but the lure of his work has been gradually too much for him, and he is now blissfully copying from one paper on to another while the measured words flow over him, his lips forming the phrases while he writes.*

WESTON. ... And furthermore (*he pauses to arrange the tobacco*), it is not alone a question of duty; there is your own success in the world to be considered. It is not your intention to be a secretary all your life, is it? No. Very well. Diligence and a respect for detail should be your care. I did not become Lord Weston by twiddling my thumbs and hoping for favours. I won my honours by hard work and zealous service. Men who were at Corpus Christi with me are today copying documents

3

for a living, while I – let us not mince matters – am the best-known, and certainly the most impartial, judge in England, and a favoured servant of his gracious majesty, Charles the Second. That, I submit, my good Roger, is an example to be studied. It is not only unbecoming in you to ask for a half-holiday, but it is greatly unlike you. I fear – (*He has turned towards his secretary, and discovers his misplaced diligence. After a pause, coldly.*) Can it be, Mr. Chetwynd, that you have not been listening to my discourse?

ROGER (*brought to the surface by the cessation of the word-music*). What, my lord? Oh, no. Yes, certainly, sir, I am listening.

WESTON. What was I talking of?

ROGER. Yourself, sir. (*Amending.*) I mean, of your rise to success, my lord.

       (*It is apparent that it is an oft-heard tale.*)

WESTON. We were talking of your extraordinary request for a half-holiday, when you had one only last month. On that occasion, if I remember well, your parents came to town and you must needs go gadding. Would it be straining courtesy too far if I were to inquire what prompts this new demand for heedless leisure?

ROGER. I thought perhaps if you did not need me this afternoon, my lord, I might personally interview the clerk of the Awards Committee, and find out why he has not sent that document.

WESTON (*a little taken aback*). Oh. Oh, indeed.

ROGER. The lack of it greatly hinders my work, you see. And at this most interesting point –

      (*His glance goes longingly to his desk.*)

WESTON. That, of course, is a different matter. I see no reason (*he looks for a spill for his pipe first on the table and then, rising, by the fire*) why you should not take a walk to Mr. Clay's in the afternoon if the weather is fine. I am relieved that your thoughts are on sober matters, as befits a rising young man. Diligence, courage, and attention to detail: these are the three – Where are the spills? These are what bring a man to success and endow him with dignity – No tapers and no spills, as usual! (*Looking on the table for a scrap of paper and finally feeling in his pockets.*) Without an orderly mind no man can hope (ROGER *has gone back to his work.*) to excel in any of the learned professions. (*He has found a scrap of paper, rather crushed, in his pocket and smooths it out, uninterestedly, to make a rough spill.*) Detail, my good Roger, attention to detail. That is the beginning of greatness. That is the – (*reading automatically and with some difficulty what is written on the scrap of paper*) 'Remember Caesar.' (*Repeating, with vague interest.*) 'Remember Caesar.' (*He turns the paper back and forth, at a loss. And then a new idea occurs to him, a rather horrible idea. To* ROGER.) What is the date today? (*As* ROGER, *buried again in his work, does not answer.*) Roger! I said, what day of the month is it?

ROGER (*hardly pausing*).   It is the fifteenth, my lord.

WESTON.   The fifteenth! The fifteenth of March. The Ides of March! (*Looking at the paper again; in a horrified whisper.*) 'Remember Caesar'! (*Louder.*) So they want to kill me, do they? They want to kill me? (ROGER *comes to the surface, surprised.*) That is what it is to be a judge over men (*all his pompousness is dissolving in agitation*), an instrument of justice. Sooner or later revenge lies await in the by-ways. And the juster a judge has been, the more fearless (*he waves the paper in the astonished* ROGER's *face*), so much greater will be the hate that pursues –

ROGER.   What is it, my lord? What is it?

WESTON.   My death warrant if I am not careful. What cases have we had lately? The treason affair – I refused to be bribed! (*The boast gives him a passing comfort.*) The piracy – both sides hate me for that! Or there was that footpad –

ROGER.   Is it a threat, the paper? Where did it come from?

WESTON.   It was in my pocket. Someone must have — Yes, now I remember. A man brushed against me yesterday as I was leaving the Courts. A small, evil-looking fellow, very sly.

ROGER.   What does it say, the paper?

WESTON (*much too occupied with his own fate to attend to his secretary's curiosity*).   Just at the door, it was, and he didn't wait for an apology. I remember. Well, I can only thank them for the warning. I may die before my time, but it will not be today if I can help it. Go downstairs at once, Roger, and lock and bar all the doors. Lock, bar, and chain them. And ask my wife to come to me at once. At once. Stop! Are there any strangers in the house? Workmen or such?

ROGER.   Only Joel the gardener, my lord; he is cleaning the windows on the landing.

(*He indicates with his head that Joel is just outside.*)

WESTON.   Send him away at once. Tell him to leave everything and go, and lock the door behind him. And the windows — see that all the windows, too, are closed.

(ROGER *goes with speed. One can hear him begin his order to Joel before he shuts the door:* Joel, his lordship says that you must ... *and the whistling which has become audible through the opened door dies away.* WESTON, *left alone, peers cautiously from each window in turn. Then his mind, temporarily relieved, goes to the cupboard and is greatly exercised again. He stares at it fearfully for a moment or two, and then puts his fear to the test. He takes a pistol from the drawer of his desk.*)

WESTON (*facing the cupboard with levelled gun*).   Come out! Come out, I say. (*There is silence.*) Drop your weapon and come out, or I shall shoot you now.

(*As there is still silence he forces himself to close in on the cupboard door, and, standing to the side, pulls it quickly open. It is empty. As soon as his relief abates he is ashamed, and hastily returns the pistol to its drawer.*)

(*Enter, bright and purposeful,* LADY WESTON. *A charming creature. One knows at a glance that she is an excellent housewife, but to the last one is never sure how much intelligence and sweet malice there lies behind her practical simplicity.*)

LADY WESTON (*looking back as she comes in*). I do wish that Joel wouldn't leave pails of water on the landing! What is it, Richard? It's baking morning.

WESTON (*going to her and taking her hand in his reassuringly*). My dear, don't be alarmed —

LADY WESTON. I'm not. But the surest way to make me is to pat my hand and tell me not to be.

WESTON. My dear, your husband's life is in grave danger.

LADY WESTON. The last time it was in danger you had been eating game pie. What is it this time?

WESTON (*annihilating her flippancy with one broadside*). Assassination!

LADY WESTON. Well, well! You always wanted to be a great man and now you have got your wish!

WESTON. What do you mean?

LADY WESTON. They don't assassinate nobodies.

WESTON (*showing her the paper*). Read that, and see if you can laugh.

LADY WESTON. I'm not laughing. (*Trying to read the writing.*) What a dreadful scrawl.

WESTON. Yes, the venomous scribbling of an illiterate.

LADY WESTON (*deciphering*). 'Remember Caesar.' Is it a riddle?

WESTON. It is a death warrant. Do you know what day this is?

LADY WESTON. Thursday.

WESTON. What day of the month.

LADY WESTON. About the twelfth, I should guess.

WESTON (*with meaning*). It is the fifteenth. The fifteenth of March.

LADY WESTON. Lawdamussy! Your good sister's birthday! And we haven't sent her as much as a lily!

WESTON. I have deplored before, Frances, the incurable lightness of your mind. On the fifteenth of March Caesar was murdered in the Forum.

LADY WESTON. Yes, of course. I remember. They couldn't stand his airs any longer.

WESTON (*reprovingly*). He was a great man.

LADY WESTON (*kindly*). Yes, my dear, I am sure he was. (*Looking again at the scrap of paper.*) And is someone thinking of murdering you?

WESTON. Obviously.

LADY WESTON. I wonder someone hasn't done it long ago. (*Before the look of wonder can grow in his eye.*) A great many people must hate judges. And you are a strict judge, they say.

WESTON. It is the law that is strict. I am a judge, my good Frances, not a juggler. I have never twisted the law to please the mob, and I shall not please them by dying on the day of their choice.

LADY WESTON. No, of course not. You shall not go out of the house today. A nice light dinner and a good glass of —

WESTON. I have sent Roger to barricade all the doors, and I think it would be wise to close the ground-floor shutters, and see that they are not opened for any —

LADY WESTON. Is it the French and the Dutch together you are expecting! And this is the morning Mr. Gammon's boy comes with the groceries. How am I to —

WESTON. My dear, is a litle pepper more to you than your husband's life?

LADY WESTON. It isn't a little pepper, it's a great deal of

flour. And you would be the first to complain if the bread were short, or the gravy thin. (*Giving him back the paper.*) How do you know that the little paper was meant for you?

WESTON. Because it was in my pocket. I found it there when I was looking for something to light my pipe. (*With meaning.*) There were no spills.

LADY WESTON. No spills. What, again? Richard, you smoke far too much.

WESTON (*continuing hastily*). It was slipped into my pocket by a man who brushed against me yesterday. A dark, lean fellow with an evil face.

LADY WESTON. I don't think he was very evil.

WESTON. What do you know about it?

LADY WESTON. It was kind of him to warn you. And wasn't it a mercy that the spills were finished and that no one had made any more! If there had been even one there you would have gone for your noon walk down the Strand and someone would have stuck you like a goose on a spit, and I should have been a widow before dinner-time —

WESTON (*sinking into a chair*). Stop, Frances, stop. It upsets me to —

> (*Enter* ROGER, *a little out of breath after his flying tour round the house.*)

WESTON. Ah, Roger. Have you seen to it all? Every door barred, every window shut, all workmen out —

ROGER (*a little embarrassed*). Every door except the kitchen one, my lord.

WESTON (*angry*). And why not the kitchen one?

ROGER (*stammering*). The cook seemed to think — That is, she said —

WESTON. Well, speak, man, what did she say, and how does what the cook thinks affect my order to bar the kitchen door?

ROGER (*in a rush*). The cook said she was a respectable woman and had never been behind bars in her life and she wasn't going to begin at her age, and she was quite capable of dealing with anyone who came to the kitchen door —

LADY WESTON. Never mind, Roger, I shall speak to Cook —

WESTON (*interrupting her, furious*). Is the woman mad? Did you tell her that her master might be killed in her very presence if the door were not —

ROGER. I did, my lord, I did. She said there would be a killing there and then if I did not leave her kitchen. She is a very formidable woman, my lord, and there was the matter of a rolling-pin ... I thought it best to desist.

LADY WESTON. Be calm, Richard. It is only that the cook's temper is apt to be uncertain in the morning. I know how to coax her into a better humour —

WESTON. Coax! Since when have my servants to be coaxed! She shall leave my house this very hour.

LADY WESTON. Oh, nonsense, Richard! All cooks are strange-tempered. It comes from standing over hot stoves and breathing in pepper. I shall see —

WESTON. This very hour! If her silly mind is so careless of her master's safety, she has no right to his roof. Tell her to pack her things and leave the house at once, and see that the door is barred after her.

LADY WESTON. And who will cook your pet dishes when I go to stay with Sibylla? Be calm, Richard. The kitchen door will be locked, and Cook will see to the barring of it herself, and be proud of her handiwork, I promise you. That is what a mistress is for, to sweep up after the master. I shall also see that all the downstairs windows are shuttered as you suggest. We can always haul the groceries through an upper window. That will be entertaining for poor old Lady Gascoigne, anyhow; glooming there in her window. She has had no amusement out of this street since the dog-fight on Ash Wednesday. (*As she is going, pausing.*) Would you like me to block up the chimneys, perhaps?

WESTON (*controlling himself*). I think that so frivolous a suggestion at so anxious a time is in poor taste, Frances, and unworthy of you —

LADY WESTON. Did it appear frivolous to you? How strange! I had thought it odd to shutter the walls and yet leave openings in the roof that one could drive a coach and horses through. However!

> (*She comes back into the room, takes two candelabra from various places about the room, and goes to the door.*)

WESTON. What do you want with these?

LADY WESTON. If we are to be in darkness below we shall want all the candles we can gather.   (*Exit.*)

WESTON. The aptness of the female mind to busy itself about irrelevant and inconsiderable minutiae is a source of endless wonder to me. (*Almost without noticing what he is doing he moves over to the fireplace and sticks his head into the chimney to view the width of it. As he withdraws it he becomes aware of* ROGER, *standing watching.*) I see no reason now why you should not resume your work, Roger.

ROGER. Oh, my lord, it is beyond my power to work while you are in danger. Is there not something I could do?

WESTON (*mightily flattered*). Nonsense, my good Roger, nonsense! Nothing is going to happen to me.

ROGER. I could perhaps go and warn the authorities, and so prevent —

WESTON (*very brave*). No, no, no. Am I to spend the rest of my life with a guard at my heels? A pretty figure I should cut! Go on with your work and — (*His eye has lighted on a package which is lying on a chair against the right wall. The box is oblong — roughly* 18 × 10 × 4 *inches — and tied with cord.*) (*Sharply.*) What is this?

ROGER. That came for you this morning, sir.

WESTON. What is it?

ROGER (*with the faint beginnings of doubt in his voice.*)   I don't know, my lord. A man came with it and said that it was important that you should have it today.

WESTON.   And you didn't ask what it was! You fool!

ROGER (*humbly*).   It didn't seem to be my business. I never do ask about the contents of your lordship's — I showed your lordship the package when it came, and you said to leave it there.

WESTON (*peering with growing uneasiness at the thing*). The man who brought it, what did he look like? Was he small? Dark?

ROGER (*who obviously had taken no notice*).   I think he was smallish. But as to dark — his hat was pulled over his face. I think, I think he appeared to have a mole on his chin, but I would not — It may have been just a —

WESTON.   A mole? (*His imagination at work.*) A mole! Yes. Yes. That man had a mole. The man who brushed against me. On the right side of his jaw. I can see it as if he were standing here. We must get rid of this. At once.

ROGER.   Do you think it is some infernal machine, sir? What shall we do with it?

WESTON (*indicating the side-window*).   Open the window, and I shall throw it as far into the garden as I can.

ROGER.   But it may explode, sir, if we throw it.

WESTON.   What is certain is that it will explode if we do not! How long has it been lying here?

ROGER.   It came about nine o'clock, my lord.

WESTON (*in an agony*).   Nearly three hours ago! Open the window, Roger.

ROGER.   No, sir. You open the window. Let me handle the thing. My life is nothing. Yours is of great value to England.

WESTON.   No, Roger, no. You are young. I have had my life. There are still great things for you to do in the world. You must live, and write my life for posterity. Do as I say. I promise you I shall exercise the greatest care. (*As* ROGER *rushes to the window*.) No. Wait! A better idea. The gardener's pail. It is still on the landing!

ROGER. Yes! Yes, of course!

> (*He is out of the room and back in a moment with the wooden pail of water, which still has the wet cleaning-rag hung over its edge.*)

WESTON. Stand back. (*He picks up the parcel gingerly.*) We do not know what satanic thing may happen. (*He inserts the parcel lengthwise into the pail at full stretch of his arm, his head averted, his eyes watching from their extreme corners.*) There is not enough water! Not enough to cover it.

ROGER. I'll get some. I shall not be a moment.

WESTON. No. Don't go. The flowers!

> (*He indicates a bowl of daffodils.*)

ROGER. Of course! (*He pulls the daffodils from their setting, throwing them on the desk in his agitation, and pours the water into the pail.*) Ah! That has done it!

WESTON (*dismayed, as he takes his hand from the package*). Now it is going to float! It must be wet through, or it is no use.

ROGER. We must put something heavy on top, to keep it down.

WESTON. Yes, yes. Get something.

ROGER. What shall I get?

WESTON. Good God, boy! Have you no ideas once the pen is out of your hand? Anything, anything that is heavy and that will fit into the pail. Books, anything!

ROGER (*to whom books are objects of reverence, if not awe*). Books, sir? But they'll get very wet, won't they?

WESTON. In the name of Heaven bring the first six books off the shelf!

ROGER (*snatching the books and bringing them*). I suppose it cannot be helped. Such beautiful bindings too!

> (*He picks the wet cloth off the edge of the pail, dropping it on the carpet, and plunges the books into the*

*water, which very naturally overflows at this new
incursion.*)

WESTON (*letting go his hold on the package and sitting
back on his heels with a sigh of relief*). Ah! Well and truly
drowned.

(*He mops his forehead, and* ROGER *collapses into the
nearest chair.*)

(*Enter* LADY WESTON, *with a tray on which is a glass of
wine and some biscuits.*)

LADY WESTON (*seeing their strange occupation*). Lawdamussy,
Richard! What have you got in the pail?

WESTON.   A package that came this morning. The man who
brought it was the same fellow that knocked against me yesterday and slipped that paper into my pocket. They thought I
would open it, the fools! (*He is beginning to feel better.*) But
we have been one too many for them!

LADY WESTON (*in wild dismay*).   But how stupid! You are
just making a mess of the beautiful, brand-new —

WESTON (*interrupting her angrily*).   Frances! (*The thunder
of her name quenches her speech.*) What does your 'beautiful
brand-new' carpet matter when your husband's life is at stake?
You shock me.

LADY WESTON (*who had not been going to say 'carpet'*). Carpet? (*After a pause, mildly.*) No, of course not, my dear. I
should never dream of weighing your safety against even the
finest product of Asia. Come and sit down and have a glass of
wine. (*She puts the tray on his desk, gathering up the scattered
daffodils as she does so.*) You know how the doctor disapproves
of excitement for you.

WESTON.   Perhaps the doctor has never had an infernal
machine handed in at his door of a spring morning.

(LADY WESTON *picks up the cloth from the floor, mops
the spilt water, and pauses to look curiously at the
contents of the pail as they catch her eye.*)

ROGER (*who has been staring at the pail in absorbed fascination*). I am afraid we have made a little mess. Please let me do that.

LADY WESTON (*in mild conversational tones*). That looks like Mr. Spencer in the water.

ROGER. Yes, it is. The thing floated, you see. And time was all-important. So it was imperative to take whatever was nearest to weight it down.

LADY WESTON. I see. (*Handing him the wet cloth and the flowers.*) Would you be kind enough to take these downstairs? (*She adds the empty flower-bowl to his load.*) One of the maids will fill it for you.

WESTON. Have the kitchen wenches decided that the door of their domain may at last be bolted?

LADY WESTON. Oh, they are all very happy. Cook thinks she knows how to make bullets by dropping hot lead into cold water, or something of the sort. And the kitchen-maid thinks that she will stay in London after all.

WESTON. Stay in London?

LADY WESTON (*indicating his tray; he is already sipping the wine*). Try the biscuits. They are Sibylla's recipe. Yes, she was leaving because she found London so quiet after the country.

WESTON (*through his biscuit*). Ridiculous!

LADY WESTON. In the country, she said, if there wasn't a calving, there was a wedding, and if there wasn't a wedding there was a wake. It was never dull. A pleasant girl. I am glad London is being livelier for her.

WESTON. My household seem to treat my danger as a sort of raree-show.

LADY WESTON. No, dear, no. All maids like a little to-do. It makes life important for them.

WESTON. A little to-do! My funeral, I hope, will be even more exciting for them. You must have a wake to please the kitchen-maid.

LADY WESTON (*not listening to him; contemplative, her eyes on the portrait which hangs opposite the side-window*). Do you think we had better remove the portrait of Great-aunt Cicely from the wall?

WESTON.   In the name of Heaven, why?

LADY WESTON.   She is in the direct line of shots coming through that window.

WESTON.   And why should any shots come through the window, may I ask?

LADY WESTON (*mildly objecting to the tone*). I was merely taking thought for your property, my dear Richard. And anyone sitting in the ilex-tree out there would be in a —

WESTON (*on his feet*).   Frances! What made you think of the ilex-tree?

LADY WESTON.   That is where I would shoot you from. I mean, if I were going to shoot you. The leaves are thick enough to hide anyone sitting there, and yet not enough to obscure their view.

WESTON.   Come away from that window.

LADY WESTON.   What?

WESTON.   Come away from that window!

LADY WESTON (*moving to him*).   No one is going to shoot *me*.

WESTON (*running out of the room, and calling to* ROGER *from the landing*).   Roger! Roger!

ROGER (*very distant*).   My lord?

WESTON.   Has the gardener gone away yet?

ROGER.   No, my lord. He is eating his dinner outside the kitchen window.

WESTON.   Tell him to sit under the ilex-tree until I give him leave to move.

ROGER.   The ilex-tree? Yes, my lord.

> (WESTON *comes back and goes to the drawer of the table where his pistol is kept.*)

LADY WESTON.   What are you looking for, Richard? (*As he*

takes out the pistol.) Oh, Richard, dear, be careful. That is a very dangerous weapon.

WESTON (*grimly important.*) I know it!

LADY WESTON. It is so rusty that it is liable to do anything. (*As her husband proceeds to load the weapon.*) You know that you haven't used it since you were shooting dancing balls off the fountain. That was the year after we were married. The butcher's son blew half his scalp off the other week, trying to fire a rusty pistol. He has no hair left except a few red tufts over the right ear. His father says the only hope for him is to become a gentleman so that he can wear a wig.

WESTON. There is nothing wrong with my pistol but a little dust.

LADY WESTON. Well, I think it is a poor way to foil an assassin.

WESTON. What is?

LADY WESTON. Blowing oneself up.

(*Enter* ROGER *with a bowl of daffodils.*)

WESTON (*looking round at him as he comes*). Ah, Roger. Has Joel gone to sit under the tree?

ROGER. Yes, sir. (*Putting down the bowl and making for the side-window.*) At least, I gave him your message.

WESTON. Keep away from that window! (*As* ROGER *looks astonished.*) There may be someone in the ilex-tree.

ROGER. But do you think they would try to shoot you as well as — as — (*He indicates the bucket.*)

WESTON. Who knows? When you have dealt with the criminal mind as long as I have — Did you open the door to speak to the gardener?

ROGER. Oh, no, my lord. I spoke through the shutter. The cook is of the opinion that we should send for the military.

LADY WESTON. Cook is always of opinion that we should send for the military.

WESTON (*snapping the lock of his pistol*).   Now, we shall see whether there is anyone lurking in the tree.

>(*He moves over to the side of the window, peering out with the fraction of an eye.*)

LADY WESTON.   Richard, if you are going to shoot off that thing, you will please wait until I —

>(*She is interrupted by a loud knocking on the front door downstairs. This is such an unexpected development that all three are momentarily quite still, at a loss. ROGER is the first to recover; he moves over to the window in the rear wall, from which one can see the street.*)

ROGER.   Someone at the front door.

>(*He is about to open the casement so that he may lean out to inspect the knocker, when LORD WESTON stops him.*)

WESTON (*still at the fireplace*).   Don't open that window!

ROGER.   But I cannot see otherwise, my lord, who it is.

WESTON.   If you put your head out of that window they may shoot without waiting to ask questions.

LADY WESTON.   But, Richard, it may be some perfectly innocent visitor.

>(*The knocking is repeated.*)

ROGER.   If I were to stand on a chair ...

>(*He brings a chair to the window and stands on it, but he is still not high enough to look down on whoever waits at the front door.*)

WESTON.   Well? Well? Can you tell who it is?

ROGER.   I am still not high enough, my lord.

LADY WESTON.   Add the footstool, Roger.

ROGER.   Ah, yes, the footstool. The footstool will do it. There!

>(ROGER *adds the footstool to the chair, and, aided by* LADY WESTON, *climbs onto the precarious erection.*)

LADY WESTON. Now, can you see anyone?

ROGER (*having seen, scrambling down*). All is well, my lord. (*He throws open the casement and calls to someone below.*) In a moment, my good sir, in a moment! All is well, my lord. It is only Mr. Caesar. (*As this information is succeeded by a blank pause.*) Shall I let him in?

WESTON. Who did you say?

ROGER. Mr. Caesar. You remember: the man you met on Tuesday at Hampton, my lord. He was to come to see you this morning about rose-trees. You made a note of it.

WESTON (*taking the crumpled piece of paper from his pocket in a dazed way*). I made a note? 'Remember Caesar.' Is that my writing? Yes, it must be. Dear me!

LADY WESTON (*considering the writing: kindly*). I shouldn't have said it was the venomous scribbling of an illiterate. You had better go down and let Mr. Caesar in, Roger. Put the pistol away, Richard dear; your visitor might misunderstand it. (*She speaks cheerfully, as to a child; it is obvious from her lack of surprise that excursions and alarms created by her husband over trifles are a normal part of existence for her.*) And if you take Mr. Spencer out of the water, I shall send Joel to take away the bucket. Perhaps Mr. Brutus would like some cordial?

WESTON. Mr. *Caesar.*   (*He moves towards the bucket.*)

LADY WESTON. Of course. How could anyone forget a name like that? And now, if you'll forgive me ... It's my busy morning.

WESTON (*arresting her as she is going out of the door*). Oh, Frances! What was in the parcel, do you think?

LADY WESTON. That was your new velvet cloak, dear. I did try to tell you, you know.   (*Exit.*)

(*The curtain comes down on* LORD WESTON *ruefully taking the first dripping book from the water.*)

THE THREE WAYFARERS

Dramatized by Thomas Hardy
from his story entitled *The Three Strangers*

CHARACTERS

The Shepherd (age 28)
The Parish Constable (age 50)
Timothy Sommers (age 30), a condemned sheep-
    stealer
Joseph Sommers (age 32), his brother
The Hangman (age 55)
The Serpent Player
A Magistrate
A Turnkey
The Shepherd's Wife
A Damsel, betrothed to the Constable
Other Peasants, male and female, guests of the
    shepherd

SCENE: *The interior of a cottage near Casterbridge, Wessex.*
TIME: *A March evening at the beginning of the last century.*

Ordinary rural furniture with case-clock, dresser, etc. Wide chimney and fire burning, left. Lighted candles on mantelpiece. Seat in chimney-corner, table and chair in front of fire. Centre of room clear for dancing. Broad small-paned window, centre. Door, centre right, another door, right up-stage. Barrel on horse, right front.

The curtain rises on a country dance of six to ten couples. Tune: 'The College Hornpipe'. Figure: Three top couples six hands round and back again. Promenade with partners once round. Down the middle and up again. Swing partners. Next couple do the same. When first couple has danced down three couples the figure starts again at top.

Dancers: SHEPHERD, SHEPHERD'S WIFE, CONSTABLE, DAMSEL, *and others of the party.* SERPENT PLAYER, BOY FIDDLER, *etc., in corner.*

Dance ceases. SHEPHERD *and* WIFE *go to barrel, bring mugs and cups, pour out and hand to dancers and musicians. Rain heard without.*

SHEPHERD. After that you must be all wishing to wet your windpipes. Here, neighbour, drink hearty.

SHEPHERD'S WIFE. And perhaps while we rest somebody will favour us wi' a song? There's no going home till morning if this weather lasts.

SERPENT PLAYER. Your house stands in the full stroke of the wind, too, up here at the top o' the down.

SHEPHERD. Ay, yes. 'Tis a bleak place we live in. But one

gets used to it in time ... Which shall it be next? Another dance or a song?

  (*A knocking heard.*)

SHEPHERD. Was that a knock?

  (*Louder knocking.*)

SHEPHERD'S WIFE. Who can it be at this time o' night and in such weather?

SHEPHERD. Walk in!

  (*Enter* TIMOTHY SOMMERS. SHEPHERD *snuffs candle and holds it up to examine visitor.*)

TIMOTHY. The rain is so heavy, friends, that I ask leave to come in and rest awhile.

SHEPHERD. To be sure, stranger. And faith, you've been lucky in choosing your time, for we're having a bit of a fling in a glad cause.

TIMOTHY. And what may be this glad cause?

SHEPHERD. A birth and a christening. To be sure, a man could hardly wish such a form of gladness to happen more than once a year.

SHEPHERD'S WIFE. Nor less. For 'tis best to get your family over and done with as soon as you can, so as to be all the earlier out o' the fag o't.

TIMOTHY. Well, I hope you and your good husband may not be made unhappy either by too many or too few of such little strangers.

SHEPHERD. *She* won't! I think I can see another in her eye already.

  (SHEPHERD'S WIFE *turns away.*)

CONSTABLE. Late to be traipsing across this coomb – hey, stranger?

TIMOTHY. Late it is, master, as you say. (*Walks aside, wiping his face.*) But those in chase of me will be later! ... Lord save me! ... I'd almost as soon have stayed to be hanged as bear the strain of this escape! (*Aside.*)

SHEPHERD.   And what's the latest news from Casterbridge, stranger? Going to hang-fair tomorrow, like other folk, I suppose?

TIMOTHY (*with a start*).   I — hadn't heard of it.

CONSTABLE.   What — not about this sheepstealer, that was tried last 'size and is waiting his awful doom in Casterbridge gaol? Yes — he's to be turned off tomorrow morning.

TIMOTHY.   I — suppose you are going with the rest?

CONSTABLE.   Well, no. As a gover'ment officer I've seen fifteen strung up, man and boy; and there's a sameness in it after a while; and 'tis bad for the nerves. Yes, his time is getting short.

SHEPHERD.   In a few hours we shall have the folk hurrying past here to get to the sight early.

SERPENT PLAYER.   'Twasn't one of your sheep that a' stole, shepherd?

SHEPHERD.   Oh, no. I haven't lost one this winter. 'Twas from some farm by Shottsford. I don't know the place at all.

SERPENT PLAYER.   Who'll do the gallus job now our hangman is dead?

CONSTABLE.   They'll have to send for a new hand, I reckon.

SHEPHERD'S WIFE.   Well, Heaven send that they let the poor man drop easy, though some die hard, that's true ...

TIMOTHY (*to* SHEPHERD'S WIFE).   I'll take a seat in the chimney-corner if you've nothing to say against it, ma'am? For I am a little moist on the side that was next the rain.

SHEPHERD'S WIFE.   Ay, sure. (*He enters chimney-corner and stretches out legs.*) Your boots are the worse for wear.

TIMOTHY.   Yes — I am rather thin in the vamp. And I am not well fitted, either. I have seen some rough times lately, and have been forced to pick up what I could get in the way of wearing but I must find a suit better fitted for working days when I get home.

SHEPHERD'S WIFE.   One of hereabouts?

TIMOTHY.   Not quite, ma'am. Further up the country.

SHEPHERD'S WIFE.   I thought so. And so be I. And by your tongue you seem to come from my neighbourhood.

TIMOTHY (*hastily*).   But you would hardly have heard of me. (*Blandly.*) My time would be long before yours, ma'am, you see ... Really, if I'd not met you here as a married woman, I should have said to 'ee 'My dear young girl!'

SHEPHERD'S WIFE (*simpering*).   Get along with thee!

TIMOTHY.   Really, I should! When was you married, ma'am? Last year?

SHEPHERD'S WIFE.   I've been married five years and have three children.

TIMOTHY.   No! Impossible! Really, married women shouldn't look such maiden deceptions. 'Tisn't moral of 'em! Why, I won't say that I shouldn't have asked to pay my addresses to 'ee if I'd been a younger fellow and as well off as I was formerly.

SHEPHERD'S WIFE.   Ah – poor man. (*To* SHEPHERD, *who has been helping guests to liquor.*) Pour out some for the stranger. I never met a civiller man.

TIMOTHY (*to* SHEPHERD).   There is only one thing more wanted to make me happy. And that a little baccy, which I'm sorry to say I'm out of.

SHEPHERD.   I'll fill your pipe.

TIMOTHY.   I must ask you to lend me a pipe likewise.

SHEPHERD.   A smoker, and no pipe about 'ee?

TIMOTHY (*confused*).   I've dropped it somewhere on the road.

SHEPHERD (*handing pipe*).   Hand me your baccy box – I'll fill that too, now I am about it. (TIMOTHY SOMMERS *searches pockets.*) Lost that, too?

TIMOTHY.   I'm afraid so. Give it to me in a screw of paper.
(*Lights pipe.*)

SHEPHERD.   Neighbours, another dance? Shall it be hands across, this time?

GUESTS. Ay, ay, maister – hands across.

SHEPHERD. Strike up, fiddler.

> (*Country dance: two top couples hands across and back again. Down the middle and up again. Swing partners. The other couples do the same.*)

SHEPHERD'S WIFE. Get the man some more mead.

> (*Knocking.* TIMOTHY SOMMERS *starts up and sits again. Dance ceases.*)

SHEPHERD. What – another?

CONSTABLE. Another visitor!

SHEPHERD. Walk in!

> (*Enter* HANGMAN, *right centre entrance – bag in hand.*)

HANGMAN. I must beg for a few minutes' shelter, comrades, or I shall be wetted to the skin before I reach Casterbridge.

SHEPHERD. Make yerself at home, master – make yerself at home; though you be a stranger.

> (HANGMAN *removes great-coat, shakes out and hangs up hat. He advances to table by chimney-corner, deposits bag thereon and sits down outside* TIMOTHY SOMMERS *who nods and hands mug. Other guests play at forfeits or some silent game.*)

HANGMAN (*drinks*). I knew it! When I walked up your garden afore coming in, and saw the hives all of a row, I said to myself, 'Where there's bees there's honey, and where there's honey there's mead.' But mead of such a truly comfortable sort as this I really didn't expect to meet my lips in my older days!

> (*Drinks again deeply.*)

SHEPHERD. Glad you enjoy it!

SHEPHERD'S WIFE (*grudgingly*). It is goodish mead, and trouble enough to make, and we can hardly afford to have it drunk wastefully ... I hardly think we shall make any more, for honey sells well, and we can make shift without such strong liquor.

HANGMAN. Oh, but you'll never have the heart! (*Drinks

again.) I love mead, when 'tis old like this, as I love to go to church o' Sundays, or relieve the poor and needy any day of the week.

TIMOTHY.   Good — very good! Ha-ha-ha!

HANGMAN (*spreading himself in chair*).   Well, well, as I say, I am going to Casterbridge and to Casterbridge I must go. I should have been almost there by this time if the rain hadn't driven me in here; and I'm not sorry for it.

SHEPHERD.   You don't live in Casterbridge, sir, seemingly?

HANGMAN.   Not as yet; I shortly mean to move there.

SHEPHERD.   Going to set up in trade, perhaps?

SHEPHERD'S WIFE.   No, no. It is easy to see that the gentle-man is rich and don't need to work at anything.

HANGMAN (*after a pause*).   Rich is not quite the word for me, dame. I do work and I must work. And even if I only get to Casterbridge by midnight I must get to work then by eight tomorrow morning ... Yes, het or wet, blow or snow, famine or sword, my day's work tomorrow must be done.

(TIMOTHY SOMMERS *droops in agitation.*)

SHEPHERD'S WIFE.   Indeed! Then in spite o' seeming, you are worse off than we?

HANGMAN.   It lies rather in the nature of my trade, men and maidens, it is the peculiarity of my business more than my poverty ... But really and truly, I must up and away, or I shan't get a lodging in the town ... There's time for one more draught of friendship before I go, and I'd perform it at once if the mug were not dry.

SHEPHERD'S WIFE.   Here's a mug of small. Small we call it, though 'tis only the first wash of the combs.

HANGMAN.   No! I won't spoil your first kindness by par-taking of your second.

SHEPHERD.   Certainly not. We don't increase and multiply every day, and I'll fill the mug wi' strong again!

(*Goes to barrel in corner.*)

SHEPHERD'S WIFE (*following him*). Why should you do this? He emptied it once, though it held enough for ten people, and now he's not content with the small but must needs call for more of the strong! And a stranger unbeknown to any of us! For my part I don't like the look o' the man at all!

SHEPHERD. But he's in the house, my dear, and tender! And 'tis a wet night, and our baby's christening! Daze it, what's a cup o' mead more or less?

SHEPHERD'S WIFE. Very well – this time then. But what's the man's calling, and where does he come from, that he should burst in and join us like this?

SHEPHERD. I don't know. I'll ask him again. (*They return to* HANGMAN, *she pouring out a very small cupful, keeping the mug at a distance.*) And as to this trade of yours, what did you say it might be?   (*To* HANGMAN.)

TIMOTHY (*affecting frankness*). Anybody may know *my* trade. I'm a wheelwright.

SHEPHERD'S WIFE. A very good trade for these parts.

HANGMAN. Anybody may know mine – if they've the wit to find it out.

CONSTABLE. You may mostly tell what a man is by his claws. Though I be a servant o' the Crown as regards my constable-ship, I be a hedge-carpenter by trade, and my fingers be as full of thorns as a pin-cushion is of pins.

(TIMOTHY SOMMERS *quickly hides his hands.*)

HANGMAN. True, But the oddity of my trade is that instead of setting a mark upon me, it sets a mark upon my customers!

SHEPHERD'S WIFE. That's strange! (*Aside.*) I don't like the man at all … (*To the other guests.*) Will somebody favour us with a song?

GUESTS (*severally*). I've got no voice … I've forgot the first verse.

HANGMAN. Well – to start the company, I'll sing one myself. (*Sings.*)

'O my trade it is the rarest one,
　　Simple shepherds all,
　My trade is a sight to see;
For my customers I tie, and take them up on high,
　And waft 'em to a far countree —
　　　(TIMOTHY SOMMERS *drops and breaks pipe in his
　　　　agitation.*)

　　　　　　　　　　　　　　　　　　　Hee-hee!

And waft 'em to a far countree!'　　　　　(*Drinks.*)

TIMOTHY (*sings*).　'And waft 'em to a far countree!'
SHEPHERD'S WIFE.　What do the man mean?
　　　(SHEPHERD *shakes head.*)
TIMOTHY.　Second verse, stranger!
HANGMAN (*sings*).
　'My tools are but common ones (*tapping bag*),
　　　Simple shepherds all.
　My tools are no sight to see;
　A little hempen string and a post whereon to swing,
　Are implements enough for me,

　　　　　　　　　　　　　　　　　　　Hee-hee!

　Are implements enough for me.'
　　　(*Pulls end of rope from bag.* TIMOTHY SOMMERS *tries to
　　　　hide agitation.*)
GUESTS (*starting*).　Oh!
　　　(DAMSEL *faints* — CONSTABLE *catches her.*)
CONSTABLE.　Oh — he's the hangman!
SEVERAL.　He's come to hang Tim Sommers at Casterbridge
gaol tomorow morning!
OTHERS.　The man condemned for sheepstealing, what we
were talking of! — the poor clockmaker who used to live at
Shottsford! His family were starving, and so he went out of
Shottsford by the high road, and took a sheep in open daylight
… He (*pointing to the* HANGMAN) is come from up the country

to do it. Then it's he who is going to have the berth here now our own man is dead!

TIMOTHY (*sings*). 'Are implements enough for me!'

    (*Clinks cups with the* HANGMAN.)

HANGMAN. Next verse. (*Sings.*)

  'Tomorrow is –' (*Knocking without.*)

    (SHEPHERD *rises.* WIFE *tries to prevent his speaking.*)

CONSTABLE. Another of 'em?

SEVERAL. What do it mean?

SHEPHERD. Walk in!

    (*Enter* JOSEPH SOMMERS, *right centre, begins wiping shoes.*)

JOSEPH. Can you tell me the way to – (*starts*). My brother Timothy – escaped – sitting with his own hangman! (*Aside.*)

HANGMAN (*sings*).

  'Tomorrow is my working day,
    Simple shepherds all,
  Tomorrow is a working day for me;
  For the farmer's sheep is slain, and the lad who did it ta'en –
    And on his soul may God ha' mercy!

                      Hee-hee!'

TIMOTHY (*waving cup, joins in*). 'And on his soul may God ha' mercy!'

    (JOSEPH SOMMERS, *aghast, staggers and nearly falls in a fit. Exit* JOSEPH SOMMERS, *slamming door.*)

SHEPHERD. What man could he be?

    (*Silence. Company stare at* HANGMAN. *Rain without.* TIMOTHY SOMMERS *smokes unconcerned. Report of a gun.*)

HANGMAN (*jumping up*). Be jiggered! (*Rope falls on floor.*) The prison gun!

TIMOTHY. What does that mean?

SHEPHERD'S WIFE. A prisoner escaped from the gaol – that's what it means!

TIMOTHY (*after a pause*). I've often been told that in this country they fire a gun at such times, but I never heard it till now.

HANGMAN. I wonder if it is *my* man?

SHEPHERD. Surely it is! And surely we've seen him! The little man who knocked at the door by now, and quivered like a leaf when he saw 'ee and heard your song!

SHEPHERD'S WIFE. Yes! His teeth chattered, and the breath went out of his body!

CONSTABLE. And his heart seemed to sink within him like stone.

OTHERS. And he bolted as if he'd been shot at.

TIMOTHY. True – true. His teeth chattered, and his heart seemed to sink, and he bolted as if he'd been shot at.

HANGMAN. I didn't notice it.

DAMSEL. We were all wondering what made him run off in such a fright, and now 'tis explained!

(*Gun at slow intervals.*)

HANGMAN. Is there a parish constable here? If so, let him step forward. (CONSTABLE *advances*, DAMSEL *abandoning him reluctantly and sobbing over back of chair*.) You are a sworn constable?

CONSTABLE. I be, sir!

HANGMAN. Then pursue the criminal at once with assistance, and bring him back. He can't have gone far.

CONSTABLE. I will, sir – I will – when I've got my staff of office. I'll go home and get it, and come sharp here, and start in a body!

HANGMAN. Staff – never mind your staff! The man'll be gone!

CONSTABLE. But I can't do nothing without my staff – can I, shepherd, and Elijah and John? No; for there's the King's royal crown a-painted on en in yaller, and gold, and the lion and the unicorn, so as when I raise en up and hit my prisoner, 'tis made a lawful blow thereby. I wouldn't attempt to take up a man without my staff – no, not I. If I hadn't the law to give me courage, why instead o' my taking him up he might take me up!

DAMSEL (*clinging to him*). Don't 'ee risk your life, dear. Don't 'ee!

HANGMAN. Now I'm a King's man myself, and can give you authority enough for this. Now then, all of ye, be ready. Have ye any lanterns?

CONSTABLE. Yes, have ye any lanterns? I demand it.

HANGMAN. And the rest of you able-bodied men –

CONSTABLE. Able-bodied men – yes – the rest of ye!

HANGMAN. Have you some good stout staves and pitch-forks –

CONSTABLE. Staves and pitchforks, in the name of the law. And take 'em in your hands and go in quest, and do as we in authority tell ye!

(*Exeunt all, right centre, except the women, with lanterns, staves, etc. Rope discovered. Start affrighted.* DAMSEL *fainting. Baby cries from another room.*)

SHEPHERD'S WIFE. Oh, my poor baby! 'Tis of ill omen for her – all this gallows work at her christening! I wouldn't have had her if I'd known!

(*Exeunt women, right up-stage. Enter stealthily* TIMOTHY SOMMERS. *Helps himself to food and drink.*)

TIMOTHY. Hunger will tame a lion – and a convict! To think they should fancy my brother the man, and not me!

(*Enter* HANGMAN, *right centre.*)

HANGMAN. Ah – you here, friend? I thought you had gone to help in the capture.

(*Staggers to mug.*)

TIMOTHY. And I thought you had.

HANGMAN. Well, on second thoughts, I felt there were enough to do it without me; and such a night as it is too.

Besides, 'tis the business of the Government to take care of its criminals till they reach my hands.

TIMOTHY.   True – so it is. And I felt, as you did, that there were enough without me.

HANGMAN.   I don't want to break my limbs running over the humps and hollows of this wild country!

TIMOTHY.   Nor I either, between you and me.

HANGMAN.   These shepherd-folk are used to it – simple-minded souls, you know – stirred up to anything in a moment. They'll have him before the morning ready for me to pinion, and turn-off – (*suiting action to word*) – and no trouble to me at all. Besides my fee, his clothes will fetch me a guinea or two, I hope, when I've stripped his corpse afore burial.

TIMOTHY.   True, true, a guinea or two for certain, when you've stripped his corpse.

HANGMAN.   By the way, I've dropped my rope somewhere. I always carry my own halter with me – the new ones they make for ye won't draw tight under the ear like an old one.

TIMOTHY.   Exactly. Not like an old one, tight under the ear! Ha-ha! Here 'tis, sir. (*Picking up rope.*)

HANGMAN.   Thank 'ee, friend. Oh, I wouldn't make a *long* strangling of it for the world. I'm too kind-hearted for that.

TIMOTHY.   Ve-ry kind-hearted-d-d-d. Ha-ha! (*Edging off.*) Good-bye. My way is –

HANGMAN.   And my way is to Casterbridge, and it is as much as my legs will do to carry me that far. Going the same way?

TIMOTHY.   No, I'm sorry to say. I've to get home over north-'ard there and I feel as you do that I must be stepping on. Good night t'ye!

HANGMAN.   Good night! Till we meet again! (*They shake hands.*)

TIMOTHY.   Till we meet again!

(*Exeunt severally. Enter* TURNKEY *and* MAGISTRATE.)

MAGISTRATE.   Nobody here?

(*Enter* SHEPHERD'S WIFE, DAMSEL *and other women.*)

SHEPHERD'S WIFE.   They are gone in pursuit, sir.

MAGISTRATE.   Ah – I think I hear them returning. Then they've caught him.

(*Enter* CONSTABLE, SHEPHERD, *musicians, other peasants, and* JOSEPH SOMMERS.)

CONSTABLE.   Gentlemen, I have brought back your man, not without risk and danger; but everyone must do his duty. I pursued him, and when I was a safe distance, I said, 'Prisoner at the bar, surrender in the name of the Saints.'

SHEPHERD.   The Crown, the Crown!

CONSTABLE.   If you had all the weight of this undertaking on your mind you'd say the wrong word perhaps! So I said, 'Surrender in the name of the Crown! We arrest 'ee on the charge of not staying in Casterbridge gaol in a decent proper manner to be hung tomorrow morning!' That's the words I said.

MAGISTRATE.   Well, well – where is the man?

CONSTABLE.   He's inside this circle of able-bodied persons, sir. Men, bring forward your prisoner!

(*They advance with* JOSEPH SOMMERS.)

TURNKEY.   Who is this man?

CONSTABLE.   The culprit!

TURNKEY.   Certainly not!

(*Re-enter* HANGMAN.)

CONSTABLE.   But how can he be otherwise? Why was he so terrified at the sight of that singing instrument of the law?

(*Pointing to* HANGMAN.)

TURNKEY.   Can't explain it. All I know is that this is not the condemned man. He's quite a different character – gaunt – dark-haired – and a voice you'd never mistake as long as you lived.

CONSTABLE.   Why, souls – 'twas the man in the chimney-corner!

SEVERAL.   Ay — 'twas the man in the chimney-corner!

MAGISTRATE.   Hey? What — haven't you got the man after all?

CONSTABLE.   Well, sir, he's the man we were in search of, that's true, and yet he's not the man we were in search of. For the man we were in search of is not the man we wanted — if you understand my everyday way, sir — for 'twas the man in the chimney-corner!

MAGISTRATE.   A pretty kettle of fish, altogether! You had better start for the other man at once.

JOSEPH.   Sir, the time has come when I might as well speak. I have done nothing; my crime is that the condemned man is my brother.

SEVERAL.   His brother!

JOSEPH.   Yes. Early this afternoon I left home to tramp to Casterbridge gaol to bid him farewell. I was benighted and called here to rest and ask the way.

HANGMAN.   Like myself.

JOSEPH.   When I opened the door I saw before me the very man, sir, my brother, Tim, that I thought to see in the condemned cell at Casterbridge. He was in this chimney-corner and jammed close to him was the executioner who had come to take his life —

HANGMAN.   According to law, according to law!

JOSEPH.   And singing a song about it, and my brother joining in to save appearances.

HANGMAN.   A deceitful rascal! How I do despise a man who won't die legal.

JOSEPH.   Tim threw a look of agony upon me, sir, and I knew it meant 'Don't reveal what you see — my life depends on it!' I was so terrified that I turned and hurried away.

MAGISTRATE.   And do you know where your brother is at present?

JOSEPH. I do not. I have not seen him since I closed the door.

CONSTABLE. I can testify to that. We kept well between 'em with our weapons, at a safe distance.

MAGISTRATE. Where does he think to fly to — what's his occupation?

JOSEPH. A watch-and-clock maker, sir.

CONSTABLE. 'A said 'a was a wheelwright — a wicked rogue!

SHEPHERD. He meant the wheels of clocks and watches perhaps. I thought his hands were whitish for his trade.

MAGISTRATE. Well, it appears to me that nothing can be gained by retaining this poor man in custody. Your business lies with the other unquestionably.

(*Enter a peasant, a boy, etc.*)

BOY. And he's gone far enough!

PEASANT. Yes — he's gone! Nobody can find he tonight, now the moon is down; and by tomorrow morning he'll be half across the Channel.

HANGMAN. 'Twas an unprincipled thing! To cheat an honest man of his perquisites, and take away his trade. How am I to live?

SHEPHERD'S WIFE. I'm unlawfully glad of it. He was a nice civil man and his punishment would have been too heavy for his sin. So brave and daring and cool as he was to sit here as he did! I pray they'll never catch him. And I hope that you, sir, will never do your morning's work at Casterbridge, or meet our friend anywhere for business purposes.

SHEPHERD. Well, neighbours, I now do hope this little dy-ver-sion is ended; and I don't see why our christening party should be cut short by such a' onseemly interruption. Another jig, friends. We don't have a baby every day!

WOMEN. God forbid!

SHEPHERD. Come then, choose your partners; form in line, and to it again till daylight.

HANGMAN. Wi' all my heart! My day's work being lost, faith, I may as well make a night of it, too, and hope for better luck at the next assizes!

SHEPHERD. Now start the tune, fiddler!

> (*They form again for the six-hands-round.* HANGMAN *tries to get each woman severally as partner, all refuse. At last* HANGMAN *dances in the figure by himself, with an imaginary partner, and pulls out rope.* JOSEPH SOMMERS *looks on pensively.*)

CURTAIN

WHAT MEN LIVE BY

An adaptation of the story by Leo Tolstoi

by

VIRGINIA CHURCH

CHARACTERS

Simon, the cobbler
Matrena, his wife
Michael, his apprentice
Baron Avedeitch, a wealthy landowner
Thedka, his footman
Sonia Ivanich, a lady of means
Brenie
Nikita
Her two adopted children, little girls of
    about six years
Anna Maloska, a widow, friend of Matrena
Trofinoff, a debtor
The Guardian Angel
A Little Devil

The play takes place in a Russian city about 1880

Scene I

About four feet below the level of the street, which is reached by a few stairs at the back leading to an outer door, is the basement occupied by SIMON. *At the right of the door, on a line with the pavement, is a long narrow window through which one may see the feet of the passers-by.* SIMON, *who does most of the cobbling for the village, knows the wayfarers by the boots which he has repaired. Under the window, placed so as to catch the meagre light, is a cobbler's bench with tools on either side. At the left of the stairs are long grey curtains forming a kind of closet in which outer wraps are hung. In the corner is a small china-closet. In the left wall is a hearth; here, over the fire, the wife cooks the meals. Two old chairs huddle near the fire as if for warmth. A table, half-concealed by a worn cloth, stands near the fireplace. Opposite the fireplace is a door leading into the inner room.*

> (SIMON, *old, slow in movement, kindly of feature, is seated at his bench, mending a pair of rough hide shoes. His wife,* MATRENA, *as brown and dry as a chip, is on a stool by the fire, mending a tattered old sheepskin outer coat. Occasionally one sees the feet of pedestrians pass by the little window.* SIMON *glances up as they throw a shadow on his table.*)

MATRENA.   And who was that went by, Simon?

SIMON.   It was Thedka, my dear Matrena. Thedka, the footman of the Barina. The side-patch on his boot has lasted well.

MATRENA.   Yes, you make them last for so long that they do not need to come to you and so you have little trade.

SIMON.   But, Matrena, I could not put on patches that would no last; then I should have no trade at all. I must do my best. That is the kind of man I am.

MATRENA.   Yes, yes, Simon, that is the kind of man you are and so this is the kind of home we have, with hardly enough flour in the bin for one baking.

SIMON.   Don't fret, Matrena. We shall not starve. God is good.

MATRENA.   Aye, God is good, but His handmen are far from the likeness in which He cast them. (*A girl trips by.*) Was that Rozinka went by?

SIMON.   No, Rozinka has not such high heels. It was Ulka, the Barina's maid.

MATRENA.   I might have guessed it, after Thedka had passed. The minx is as hard on his footsteps as a man's shadow on a sunny day. It's a pity, since you shoe all the servants in the Baron's household, that the master would not let you make boots for him.

SIMON.   The boots of the nobilities are brought from Paris, and are cut from northern leather. Trofinoff told me he brought five pair from the station on his last trip.

MATRENA.   Trofinoff, h'm! Did you not tell me Trofinoff promised to come this afternoon to pay the eight roubles he has owed you three years coming Michaelmas?

SIMON.   Aye, so he said.

MATRENA.   So he said, but I'll warrant we never see a hair of his beard till he's come barefoot again. Now (*holding up the sheepskin*) I've done all I can do to your sheepskin. It's so thin the cold doesn't have to seek the holes to creep in: it walks through. It's thankful I'll be when we can buy another skin so that I can get out of the house the same time you go.

SIMON.   We'll buy a skin this very afternoon, my dear. When Trofinoff brings me the eight roubles, we shall add it to the three you have saved, and that ought to buy a good skin — if not a tanned one, at least a good rough one.

MATRENA.   *If* Trofinoff brings the money.

SIMON. He'll bring it, or, by Heaven, I'll have the cap off his head, so I will. That is the kind of man I am.

MATRENA. If he were to come in and tell you he is hard up, you would tell him not to worry his head about the roubles, that God is good.

SIMON. No, I shall say, 'Am I not hard up as well?'

MATRENA. Very well, if he comes we shall see what kind of man you are. Who was that?

SIMON. It was your friend, Anna Maloska, who wears shoes too small for her.

MATRENA. She wore large shoes after she caught her husband; but now he is dead, she wears small shoes again to catch another.

SIMON. I wonder that she did not stop.

MATRENA. She will stop on her way back from market, for there will be more news.

SIMON (*looking out of the window and rising happily*). But see here, Matrena, you wronged the good Trofinoff. He has come to pay the eight roubles, as he promised. (*There is a halting knock at the door.*) Coming! Coming! (*He limps slightly as he hastens up the steps.*)

MATRENA (*as she crosses to go into the room at the right*). Well, Simon, I shall be the last to be sorry if your faith has been rewarded.

> (*She goes out as* SIMON *opens the door to the street. He comes down with* TROFINOFF, *a middle-aged, sharp-faced little man with grey beard and keen, roving eyes. He carries a bundle wrapped in brown cloth.*)

SIMON. Welcome, Trofinoff. I salute you.

TROFINOFF. Welcome, fellow brother. I wish you everything that is good.

SIMON. I thank you, brother. Is all well at home?

TROFINOFF. Not as well as might be, alas! Fuel takes much money these days. I have a flat purse.

SIMON.　Then it was doubly good of you, friend Trofinoff, to come to settle our account. My good wife has not a kaftan or a sheepskin to wear when it snows.

TROFINOFF.　I regret, Simon, I was unable to bring you the roubles I owe you. I am so hard pressed.

SIMON (*with forced sternness*).　Am I not hard up as well?

TROFINOFF.　Aye, but you have not so many mouths to fill, nor cattle to feed, nor grain to dispose of with little profit.

SIMON.　Friend Trofinoff, you have a hut and cattle, while I have all on my back. You grow your own bread; I have to buy mine. If you do not pay me, I shall not have money for bread.

TROFINOFF.　You are not so grieved as I, brother; and had it been anyone but you I should not have dared face him, but I knew the kind of man you are. I have heard you say, 'Let us love one another.'

SIMON.　That is so, for love is of God.

TROFINOFF.　So I said to my wife: 'Anya, if it were anyone but Simon, the good Simon, I would not dare to take him our little one's shoes, but I know what kind of man he is: he loves the children and would not that the least of these should suffer and he could help it.'

　　　　(*He unwraps a tattered pair of shoes, belonging to a child.*)

SIMON.　Aye, the little Sarah's shoes. They need soles badly, and a toe-cap.

TROFINOFF.　You will repair them for her, Simon?

SIMON.　Of course, brother, I – (*He looks nervously towards the door to the inner room.*) Could you not pay me something, Trofinoff?

TROFINOFF.　Here are two copecks. They will buy a half loaf for the wife, Simon. (*He goes to the door.*)

SIMON.　Thank you.

TROFINOFF.　And you shall have your roubles in a day or so – as soon as my grain is paid for.

SIMON. I can get along very comfortably. While one of us has a warm coat, why should we fret? I can stay in by the fire. Only, of course, there's my wife. She keeps worrying about it.

TROFINOFF. Your wife has no cause to be anxious while she has such a kind husband, Simon. I will send for the boots shortly. Good day.

SIMON. Good day. God be with you, brother!

(TROFINOFF *goes out.* SIMON *lays the copecks on the bench, and is examining the small shoes when* MATRENA *enters. He puts them behind his back guiltily.*)

MATRENA. Well, what are you hiding there? Did he bring you a gift with your money?

SIMON (*sadly*). No, he — he assured me he was quite destitute.

MATRENA (*enraged*). Do you mean he brought you not even your eight roubles? (SIMON *shakes his head.*) What did I tell you, eh?

SIMON. But he says he will bring them soon — when his money comes in. I railed at him, Matrena. I scored him roundly for not paying his just dues.

MATRENA. And what have you there? (SIMON *produces the shoes and* MATRENA *is further enraged.*) I thought as much. You've taken more work for the cheater. You let him hoodwink you out of your senses while your old wife may go hungry and cold? What's this?

SIMON. He gave me two copecks for bread.

(MATRENA *hurls them angrily on the floor at* SIMON's *feet. The old man patiently picks them up.*)

MATRENA. Bread, bah! It would not buy half a loaf. The thief! It is a shame, a shame!

(*She rocks herself, crying, then falls into a chair by the fire, her apron thrown over her head, and gives way to grief.*)

SIMON (*distressed*).   Come now, Matrena, why will you wag your tongue so foolishly? If we have bread for the day, the morrow will provide for itself. As for the coat, I shall go to Vanya, the vender of skins, and get one on credit.

> (*The* LITTLE DEVIL *peers in at the window, then disappears.*)

MATRENA.   And who would give the likes of us credit with not a dessiatine of land to our share?

SIMON (*putting the shoes on the bench and preparing for outdoors.*)   Vanya will. I have bought many skins from him for my shoes. I have favoured him in his turn.

MATRENA.   Men forget past favours in the face of present desires. But if you are going out, you had better put my woollen jacket under your kaftan. The wind is bitter cold today.

> (*She goes to the curtains to the left of the stairs and takes down a close-fitting woollen sack. From a shelf of the cupboard she lifts a jar and shakes into her hand some money.* SIMON *is drawing on woollen slippers over his shoes. He puts on* MATRENA'S *jacket, a woollen kaftan or smock over it, and throws the sheepskin about his shoulders. On his bald head he draws down a fur cap.*)

SIMON (*submitting to* MATRENA'S *ministrations*).   Thank you, Matrena, I shall feel quite warm in this old sheepskin. I shan't want a new one in a lifetime.

> (*He goes up the steps.*)

MATRENA.   You won't get one, the way you conduct your business. Now, Simon, here are our three roubles; give these to Vanya on account and he should then let you have the skin.

SIMON.   He will, wife, he will.

MATRENA.   Now go, and mind you do not stop for vodka on the way — your tongue is loose enough as it is. And do not talk aloud to yourself, as is your custom, for if a thief learn you have the roubles, he will not be above killing you for them.

SIMON. God is my protection. May His good angel guard our house in my absence! Good day, Matrena!

MATRENA. Good day, Simon!

> (*He goes out, closing the door. She looks after him affectionately, then goes to the closet and taking an iron pot from the shelf, hangs it before the fire. Seeing that all is well, she crosses and goes into the inner room. The basement is but dimly lighted. The* LITTLE DEVIL, *after peering through the window to see that the coast is clear, comes in from the street, closing the door after him. He moves quickly and is merry, as if about to reap some reward for his efforts. From out of the curtains, by the stairs, steps the figure of the* GUARDIAN ANGEL *in long, flowing garments. The* ANGEL *remains in the shadows and is never clearly visible.*)

ANGEL. Why are you here?

> (*The* DEVIL *goes to the hearth and sits in front of the fire. He shows no surprise at being spoken to by the* ANGEL, *and does not look in his direction.*)

DEVIL. To try my luck to see if I can win old Simon with my dice. He has begun to ask credit, and if he stop for vodka, as I shall see that he does, that will be one more step in my direction.

ANGEL. His faith is strong.

DEVIL. So are my dice, ha! ha! (*He throws them.*) Three, six, nine! Good! The three means that he will have a little luck; it will make him drink vodka and forget his wife. Six, he will prosper, and when a man prospers in *this* world he forgets the next. Nine, nine, that is not so well. Nine means that I shall get him – if – yet 'ifs' are so little in my way. So I shall get him, unless –

ANGEL. Unless?

DEVIL (*rising*). Unless a greater than thou come into his home to protect him.

ANGEL. I am his Guardian Angel.

DEVIL (*on the stairs*). I will make the roubles jingle in his pockets so that he shall not hear the voice of the Guardian Angel. If nine had been twelve — but we shall see. I am off now to the home of the Baron, who long ago drowned the voice of his angel in vodka. I mixed his first glass. There was fox's blood to make him grow cunning, wolf's blood to make him grow cruel, and swine's blood to turn him into a pig. On my way, I shall mix a glass for Simon, to bring up in him all the beast-blood there is.

ANGEL. His faith is great.

> (*The* DEVIL *laughs derisively as he goes out and slams the door, and the* ANGEL *disappears again in the shadows. Feet go by the window and voices are heard. Then, just as* MATRENA *comes in and goes to the fire, there is a knock.*)

MATRENA. Come in. (*A comely woman of middle age enters. She is rather overdressed in poor clothes that strive to imitate the rich. It is* ANNA MALOSKA.) Ah, Anna, is it you? I thought I smelled smoke and came to tend our fire. Come in.

ANNA (*sniffing*). It smells like sulphur. That's bad luck. Who was it went out?

MATRENA. No one. Sit down. Simon has gone to buy a sheepskin. Is it cold out?

ANNA (*sitting and throwing back her wraps*). Bitter cold. It was on just such a day my poor husband caught pneumonia.

MATRENA (*sitting on the other side of the fire and tending the porridge*). I do hope Simon won't catch cold and I do hope the sheepskin-seller won't cheat him. That man of mine is a regular simpleton.

ANNA (*patting her hair*). They all are, poor dears!

MATRENA. Simon never cheats a soul himself, yet a little child can lead him by the nose. It's time he was back; he had only a short way to go.

ANNA. If it were poor dear Ivan, I should know he had stopped for a glass of vodka.

MATRENA (*walking to the window and looking out*). I hope he hasn't gone making merry, that rascal of mine.

ANNA. Ah, Matrena, they are all rascals. Ivan drank himself into a drunken stupor every evening; then he would come home and beat me, and beat little Fifi, my dog; but I have to remember that he was a man and men are like that. I shall never be happy again, now that he is in his grave. (*She weeps.*)

MATRENA (*patting her shoulder*). There, there, poor Anna!

ANNA (*brightening*). Do you like my hat?

MATRENA. Aye, aye, it is very tasty; though, if I might say, a trifle youthful.

ANNA. Why shouldn't a woman cheat Father Time if she can? He's the only man she can get even with. He liked my hat.

MATRENA. Ivan?

ANNA. Oh, no, the poor dear died without seeing it. I mean Martin Pakhom. I just met him at the door and he said, 'Good day, Anna, what a beautiful hat that is you're wearing!'

MATRENA. They say Martin drinks like a trout.

ANNA. Ah, they all do, poor dears. (*Gathering up her basket.*) I must go on. Fifi will be wanting his supper, though neither of us has eaten anything since poor Ivan died. Fifi is so affectionate. We both cry an hour every morning. Sonka times us.

MATRENA. Poor Anna!

ANNA. Won't you walk a way with me?

MATRENA. Simon went out with all our clothes upon him and left me nothing to wear. Besides, I must have his supper ready, and clean out my sleeping-room.

ANNA (*at the stairs*). I wish *I* had someone to get supper for.

(*She goes up to the door.*) Matrena, Martin said something rather pointed just now.

MATRENA.   What did he say, Anna?

ANNA.   He said, 'Marriage is a lottery!'

MATRENA.   Aye, aye, so it is.

ANNA.   I was just wondering —

MATRENA.   Yes?

ANNA.   I was wondering if Martin were thinking of taking a chance. Good-bye, Matrena.

> (ANNA *goes out.* MATRENA, *stirring her porridge, sits near the fire. The feet of two men pass the window. They belong to* SIMON *and a stranger. The men enter. The stranger is a young man, tall and slender, with fine clear-cut features and a mild, gentle expression. He is without stockings, being clad in* SIMON'S *woollen slippers and kaftan. He stands hesitating at the foot of the steps.* MATRENA *has risen and regards the two men angrily.* 'What tramp is this now, Simon has brought home?' *she is wondering.*)

SIMON.   Well, Matrena, here we are home again. (*The old man approaches his wife fearfully.* MATRENA, *after a scathing glance, turns her back on him, and tends her fire.*) We have brought our appetites with us. Get us some supper, will you? (*He takes off his sheepskin and cap, but still* MATRENA *does not respond. He motions the stranger to a chair at right.*) Sit you down, brother, and we will have some supper. Have you anything cooked that you could give us?

MATRENA (*facing him in rage*).   Yes, I have something cooked, but not for you. I can see you have drunk your senses away. (*He starts to protest.*) Do you think I cannot smell your breath? Where is our sheepskin? Did you drink up all the three roubles?

> (SIMON *goes to the stranger and reaching in the pocket of the kaftan, takes out the roubles.*)

SIMON.   No. Matrena, I did not get the sheepskin, because the vender would not let me have one unless I brought all the money. 'Bring all the cash,' he said, 'and then you can pick what skin you like. We all of us know how difficult it is to get quit of a debt.' But here are your roubles; I spent only the two copecks for the merest drop to send the blood bubbling finely in my veins.

MATRENA (*eyeing the man*).   I have no supper for a pair of drunkards like you. One cannot feed every drunkard that comes along when one has not enough in the pot for two.

SIMON.   Hold your tongue, Matrena. Give me time to explain.

MATRENA.   How much sense am I likely to hear from a drunken fool, indeed! My mother gave me some linen – and you drank it away! You go out to buy a sheepskin and drink that away, too.

SIMON.   But I did not –

MATRENA (*beside herself with rage*).   Give me my jacket! It's the only one I have, yet you sneak it off while I stay home for lack of clothes. (*As she snatches off the jacket and starts to the other room, her anger is burning off.*) You – you haven't told me who this fellow is.

SIMON.   If you will give me a chance for a word, I will. I saw this man lying by the chapel yonder, half naked and frozen. It is not summer time, you must remember. God led me to him, else he must have perished. The Baron Avedeitch drove up and I thought he would stop, but he did not. I started on, saying to myself the man could be up to no good there and if I went back I might be robbed and murdered. Then I said, 'Fie, Simon, for shame! Would you let a man die at your very door for want of clothing and food?' What could I do? I shared with him my covering and brought him here. Calm your temper, Matrena, for to give way to it is sinful! Remember we would all die, were it not for God.

(MATRENA *turns back from the door, sets a teapot on the table and pours some kvass, laying knives and forks by the plates and serving the porridge.*)

MATRENA.   Here is kvass and porridge. There is no bread. (*They eat humbly.* MATRENA *stops before the stranger.*) What is your name?

MICHAEL (*lifting his serious eyes to her face*).   Michael.

MATRENA.   Where do you come from?

MICHAEL.   From another part than this.

MATRENA.   How did you come to the chapel?

MICHAEL.   I cannot say.

MATRENA.   Someone must have assaulted you, then?

MICHAEL.   No, no one assaulted me. God was punishing me.

SIMON.   Of course, all things come from God. Yet where were you bound for?

MICHAEL.   For nowhere in particular.

SIMON.   Do you know any trade?

MICHAEL.   No, none.

MATRENA (*her heart warming within her*).   You could learn. I know, Simon, he could learn, if you would teach him. He might stay with us. There is enough straw for another bed in the hallway.

MICHAEL.   The Lord be good to you! I was lying frozen and unclothed, when Simon saw and took compassion on me. He shared with me his clothing and brought me hither. You have given me food and drink and shown me great kindness.

MATRENA.   No, I was not kind. I am ashamed of myself. (*She goes to the cupboard and brings out the one bit of bread.*) And I lied. I said there was no bread. There is one crust and you shall have half.

MICHAEL.   But you?

MATRENA (*gently*).   Eat, we shall have enough. You are

welcome to stay with us as long as you wish. (MICHAEL *turns and smiles radiantly on her.*) Let us eat.

MICHAEL.   God's blessing on this house!

Scene II

There is an air of greater prosperity than before. The cobbler's bench is new. There are flowers in the window-box and on the mantel. It is spring outside. The sound of hammering is heard within.

> (*The outer door opens and* MATRENA *enters with* ANNA MALOSKA. *The women have been to market.* MATRENA *is well, though quietly, dressed;* ANNA *in bright colours.*)

MATRENA.   Come in, Anna.

ANNA.   The men are not here. I wished to ask Simon about my shoes.

MATRENA.   They are inside, building another room. We have needed it since Michael came. Michael made the new bench.

ANNA.   Michael seems to do everything well. Just like poor Ivan.

MATRENA (*enthusiastically*).   Ah, he is wonderful! Everything that Simon teaches him he learns readily. The first day he learned to twine and twist the thread — no easy task for the apprentice. The third day he was able to work as if he had been a cobbler all his life. He never makes mistakes, and he eats no more than a sparrow. (*They sit down at the table.*)

ANNA.   He is woefully solemn.

MATRENA.   Aye, he works all day, only resting for a moment

to look upward. He never wishes to go out of doors; never jests, nor laughs. He has smiled only once: it was the night he came.

ANNA.   Has he any family — a wife?

MATRENA.   He never speaks of his own affairs.

ANNA.   *I* should manage to worm it out of him, trust me. Martin shall have no secrets that I don't know.

MATRENA.   When are you to marry, Anna?

ANNA.   Next month. It will be such a relief to let down. I shan't wear these tight stays any longer, nor such close boots. I can go to breakfast in my old wrapper and curl-papers. Now Martin has a way of dropping in to breakfast and I have to keep on my sleekest dress.

MATRENA.   Martin was in for shoes last week.

ANNA.   Yes, he says no one sews so strongly and so neatly as Michael.

MATRENA.   People come to Simon from all the country around. Since Michael came his business has increased tenfold.

ANNA.   Aye, Martin says the fame of Simon's apprentice has crept abroad. (*Regarding her own shoes.*) Martin has small feet. He told me last night he wore a number seven. But I must go.

MATRENA.   Here comes Simon now.

> (SIMON *and* MICHAEL *enter from the right. The latter is in simple workman's clothes. He bows gravely without speaking and going to the bench bends over his work.* SIMON *approaches the women, who have risen.*)

SIMON.   Ah, Anna Maloska, how fares the bride today?

ANNA.   Well, thank you, Simon. I came to order some new shoes.

SIMON.   Good, Anna. Shall we make them on the same last as before? Sixes, I believe?

ANNA.   No, Simon, I wish sevens this time. Good-bye, Matrena. Good-bye, Simon.

SIMON *and* MATRENA. Farewell, Anna.

MATRENA. Come in again, Anna.

ANNA (*at the door.*) Simon, are Martin's shoes finished?

SIMON. No, Anna, but don't worry; they will be. I had to send for more leather. He wears large boots, you know.

ANNA (*turning on the steps*). Large? Sevens?

SIMON. Elevens, Anna.

ANNA. Elevens – why – after all, Simon, I believe you may make my shoes nines. (*She opens the door.*)

SIMON. Very well, Anna.

ANNA (*looking out, becomes greatly excited*). Oh, Matrena, a fine gentleman in a great-coat is getting out here. He has two coachmen and a footman. I think it is the Baron. I must run out of his way.

> (*She disappears.* SIMON *and* MATRENA *together look out of the window.*)

MATRENA. It is the Baron Avedeitch, isn't it, Simon?

SIMON. There is no mistaking the Baron, and he is coming here.

> (*The door has been left open and is presently filled by a huge form that has to bow his great head to enter the low portal. The* BARON *has a ruddy, bibulous countenance, a neck like a bull's, and a figure of cast iron. He straightens up just inside the door.*)

BARON (*in a loud, pompous tone*). Which of you is the master bootmaker?

SIMON (*stepping aside*). I am, your honour.

BARON (*calling out of the door*). Hi, Thedka! Bring me the stuff here. (*He comes down into the room, followed by* THEDKA, *who places the bundle on the table.*) Untie it. (*The footman does so, disclosing two sheets of leather. He then withdraws.* MATRENA *curtsies every time anyone looks in her direction though no one heeds her.*) Look here, bootmaker. Do you see this?

SIMON. Yes, your nobility.

BARON. Do you know what it is?

SIMON. It is good leather.

BARON (*thundering for emphasis*). Good leather, indeed! You blockhead, you have never seen such leather in your life before. It is of northern make and cost twenty roubles. Could you make me a pair of boots out of it?

SIMON. Possibly so, your honour.

BARON. 'Possibly so!' Well, first, listen. I want a pair of boots that shall last a year, will never tread over, and never split at the seams. If you can make such boots, then set to work and cut out at once; but if you cannot, do neither of these things. I tell you beforehand that if the new pair should split or tread over before the year is out, I will clap you in prison.

MATRENA. Oh, your honour!

BARON (*ignoring her*). But, if they should not do so, then I will pay you ten roubles for your work.

SIMON (*turning to* MICHAEL). What do you think about it, brother?

MICHAEL. Take the work, Simon.

SIMON. Very well, sir.

BARON (*he sits and extends his foot*). Hi—Thedka. (THEDKA *advances and draws off the boot. The* BARON *then motions to* SIMON. MICHAEL *has advanced.*) Take my measure. (MICHAEL *kneels and takes the measure of the sole and of the instep. He has to fasten on an extra piece of paper to measure the calf, as the muscles of the* BARON's *leg are as thick as a beam.*) Take care you don't make them too tight in the leg. (*As* MICHAEL *draws back,* THEDKA *replaces the boot on his master's foot, then withdraws again to the door. The* BARON *indicates* MICHAEL.) Who is this you have with you?

SIMON. That is my skilled workman who will sew your boots.

BARON (*standing and stamping into his boot*). Look you

sharp, then, and remember this — that you are to sew them so that they will last a year. (MICHAEL *does not respond but stands gazing past the* BARON *as though he saw someone back of him. His face suddenly breaks into a smile and he brightens all over. The* BARON, *irritated, glances back of him, then scowls at* MICHAEL.) What are you grinning at, you fool? I see no one back of me to grin at. You had better see that the boots are ready when I want them. (*He stalks up the steps.*)

MICHAEL.   They will be ready when you need them.

> (*The* BARON *goes out.* THEDKA *follows, closing the door.*)

MATRENA.   What a man!

SIMON.   He is as hard as a flint stone.

MATRENA.   Why wouldn't he get hardened with the life he leads? Even death itself would not take such an iron rivet of a man.

SIMON (*taking the leather to* MICHAEL *at the bench*). Well, Michael, we have undertaken the work and we must not go amiss over it. This leather is valuable stuff.

MATRENA.   And the gentleman is short-tempered.

SIMON.   Aye, there must be no mistakes. You have the sharper eyes, as well as the greater skill in your fingers, so take these measures and cut out the stuff, while I finish sewing those toe-caps.

MICHAEL.   I will make them according to your needs.

> (*The men sit working while* MATRENA *busies herself with the housework.*)

MATRENA.   Oh, Simon, I forgot to tell you, Sonia Ivanich is coming by to get shoes for her two little girls. The little Nikita is hard to fit, but Madame has heard that Michael can fit even a lame foot.

> (MICHAEL *drops his work and leans forward.*)

MICHAEL.   A lame child?

MATRENA   Yes, poor little thing — but hush, I hear the

clamp, clamp of a wooden foot. Come, Simon, and greet her. Madame has money; you are getting all the best trade now.

> (SIMON *puts down his work and comes forward.* MATRENA *hastens up to the door and holds it open. A gentle, good-looking lady enters with* NIKITA *and* BRENIE, *two pretty little girls. They have round, wide eyes, rosy cheeks, and wear smart little shawls and dresses.*)

SONIA.   Good day to you, mistress.

MATRENA.   The same to you, madame, and the young misses. Won't you sit down?

> (SONIA *sits by the table, the two little girls burying their faces in her skirt from timidity. She pats them tolerantly.* MICHAEL *keeps regarding them, though he works.*)

SONIA.   Thank you. Is this Master Simon?

SIMON.   It is, mistress. What can we do for you?

SONIA.   I wish a pair of boots made for each of these little girls to wear for the spring.

SIMON.   Very well, madame. Will you have them leather throughout or lined with linen?

SONIA.   I believe linen will be softer. (*Lame* NIKITA *has slipped over to* MICHAEL *and he takes her on his knee.*) Well, will you see Nikita? I have never known her to take to a stranger so.

MATRENA.   All the children love Michael. He is Simon's skilled workman. He will take the measures.

> (MICHAEL *measures the little feet.* NIKITA *pats his head.*)

NIKITA.   I love you. Have you a little girl?

MICHAEL (*gently*).   No, I have no little girl.

SONIA.   Take both sets of measures from this little girl and make one *baskmak* for the crooked foot and three ordinary ones. The two children take the same size: they are twins.

MATRENA. How came she to be lame? Such a pretty little lady.

SONIA. Her mother, when dying, fell over her.

MATRENA (*surprised*). Then you are not their mother.

SONIA. No, I adopted them. But I love them as much as though they were my own, and they are as happy as the day is long; they know no difference.

SIMON. Whose children were they?

SONIA. The children of peasants. The father died on a Tuesday from the felling of a tree. The mother died that Friday, just after the twins were born. She was all alone, and in her death agony she threw herself across the baby and crushed its foot. When we found her she was stiff in death, but the children were alive.

MATRENA. Poor little mother!

SONIA. I was the only one in the village with a young child, so they were given to me to nurse. God took my own little one unto Himself, but I have come to love these like my own flesh. I could not live without them. They are to me as wax is to the candle.

SIMON. It is a true saying which reads, 'Without father and mother we may live, but without God – never.'

> (*All are drawn to look at* MICHAEL *who, sitting with his hands folded on his knees, is gazing upward and smiling as though at someone unseen by the others.*)

SONIA (*rising*). Good day, master! Come, Nikita, we shall stop in again to try the boots.

SIMON. In seven days, mistress. We thank you.

NIKITA. Good-bye, man!

MICHAEL. Good-bye, little one!

SONIA. Well, I never! The little dear!

> (*She goes out with the children.*)

SIMON. Michael, if you will bring me the awl from the

other room, I, too, will work. (*He approaches the bench as* MICHAEL *goes into the other room for the awl. He suddenly cries aloud in dismay.*) What has he done? What can ail the fellow?

MATRENA. What is it? (*She hastens to his side.*)

SIMON (*groaning*). Oh! How is it that Michael, who has lived with me for a whole year without making a single mistake, should now make such a blunder as this? The Baron ordered high boots and Michael has gone and sewn a pair of soleless slippers and spoiled the leather.

MATRENA (*aghast*). Michael has done this!

SIMON. Alas! yes, and you heard what the gentleman said. I could replace an ordinary skin, but one does not see leather like this every day. (MICHAEL *returns with the awl.*) My good fellow, what have you done? You have simply ruined me! The gentleman ordered high boots, but what have you gone and made instead? (*Before* MICHAEL *has a chance to respond, there is a loud knock at the door.*) Come in!

(*The door is opened and* THEDKA, *the footman of the* BARON, *enters.* SIMON *pushes the slipper behind him.*)

THEDKA. Good day to you!

SIMON (*uneasily*). Good day! What can we do for you?

THEDKA. My mistress sent me about the boots.

SIMON. Yes? What about them?

(MICHAEL, *unseen by the others, goes into the other room.*)

THEDKA. My master will not want them now. He is dead.

MATRENA. What are you saying?

THEDKA. He died on the way home. When we went to help him alight, he lay limp as a meal-sack on the floor of the carriage.

MATRENA. God help us!

THEDKA. My mistress sent me to tell the bootmaker to use

the leather for a pair of slippers for the corpse and to make them as quickly as he can.

> (MATRENA *and* SIMON *look at each other with wonderment in their eyes. They turn to where* MICHAEL *stood by the inner door, but he has disappeared.*)

SIMON.   You shall have them in an hour.

THEDKA.   I shall return. Good day, my master, and good luck to you!

SIMON.   And to you!

> (THEDKA *goes out, leaving* SIMON *and* MATRENA *gazing at each other in awe.*)

MATRENA.   Michael is no ordinary being. We might have guessed before this.

SIMON.   You remember how he smiled?

MATRENA.   He has smiled three times.

SIMON.   Let us see what he is doing.

MATRENA.   You do not suppose he would go from us without a word, do you?

> (*They go into the other room. Immediately the* LITTLE DEVIL *appears in the doorway at the back and the* GUARDIAN ANGEL *is seen in the shadow of the curtains at the left.*)

ANGEL.   You have lost!

DEVIL (*with a stamp of his foot*).   I have lost Simon's soul, but I have the Baron. He shall be my torch this night in hell.

ANGEL.   The faith of Simon was great.

DEVIL.   *Thou* didst not save him!

ANGEL.   One greater than I saved Simon. It was God!

> (*At the word, the* DEVIL *stamps his foot again, slams the door, and goes. The* ANGEL *disappears. From the other room come* MATRENA *and* SIMON, *crossing to the hearth.*)

SIMON.   He was in prayer.

MATRENA.   His face was illuminated, and such a light shone

from him that at first I thought it was a fire. Oh, Simon, who is this that has dwelt with us?

(MICHAEL *comes in from the other room; goes to the steps, where he turns and faces them.*)

MICHAEL.   God has pardoned me, good master and mistress. Do you also pardon me?

SIMON.   Tell us, Michael, who you are and why God punished you.

MICHAEL.   I was an angel in Heaven and God punished me because I disobeyed Him. He sent me to earth to bear away a woman's soul. But the woman, who had given birth to twin babies, cried to me, 'Angel of God, I cannot leave them! They will die. I have no kin to care for them. Do not take away my soul. Children cannot live without mother or father!' So I hearkened to the mother and flew back to God, saying, 'Little children cannot live without mother or father, so I did not take away the mother's soul.' Then God said to me, 'Go thou and fetch away the soul of the childing woman, and before thou return to Heaven thou shalt learn three words. Thou shalt learn both what that is which dwelleth in men, and what that is which is not given to men to know, and what that is whereby men live. When thou hast learned these words thou mayest return to Heaven.'

MATRENA.   Tell us what you did, Michael.

MICHAEL.   I went to earth and took the soul of the childing woman, then I rose above the village and tried to bear the soul to God, but a wind caught me, so that my wings hung down and were blown from me. The soul returned alone to God, while I fell to earth along the roadside.

(SIMON *and* MATRENA *marvel;* SIMON *speaks.*)

SIMON.   Tell me, Michael, why you smiled three times, and what were the three words of God.

MICHAEL.   When you, Simon, took me to your home and Matrena's heart prompted her to share her last crust, I smiled because I knew the first word of God. 'Thou shalt learn what that is which dwelleth in men,' and I knew by your goodness that what dwelleth in men is love. I felt glad that God had seen fit to reveal this to me, and I smiled.

MATRENA. What was it you saw over the shoulder of the Baron that made you smile?

MICHAEL. I saw the Angel of Death. No one else saw him, and I thought: Here is this man planning for boots that shall last a year, when he is to die before the nightfall. Then I smiled when I remembered that God had said, 'Thou shalt learn what it is not given to men to know.'

SIMON. What was it made you smile at the story of the good Sonia Ivanich?

MICHAEL. I recognized in the children the twins that I had thought would die. Yet this woman had fed them and loved them. In her I beheld love and pity of the living God, and I understood what that is whereby men live. And I smiled. This much do I tell you to repay your kindness: that men only appear to live by taking thought of themselves; in reality, they live by Love alone. He that dwelleth in Love dwelleth in God and God in him; for God is Love.

> (*The room is suddenly black with night. Then a hymn bursts forth as though from a great choir of voices, and in the dorway* MICHAEL, *bathed in light, stands looking upward. Before him, at the foot of the stairs, kneel the two peasants.*)

CURTAIN

PROTEST

by

NORMAN WILLIAMS

CHARACTERS

The Grandmother
The Mother
The Father
The Daughter

TIME: 1900

SETTING: The main room of a Japanese home. It is bright
and airy with walls consisting of light-coloured
wooden panels. There are entrances at left, at
right, and at centre back. In the back wall, left at
centre, is a gilded Buddhist shrine. To the right
and down-stage are the low, black tables and
cushions which represent the dining-furniture of
the Japanese household. To the left and looking
incongruously out of place is the only piece of
western furniture in the room, a plain wooden
chair. At front, left, are two floor cushions

The stage is momentarily empty. Then, from centre back, the GRANDMOTHER *enters. She is a tiny, dignified lady of advanced years. She carries a bowl and crosses the room to add it to those already on the tables. As she bends to do so, she catches sight of the chair, left, drops the dish with a crash and retreats with a shrill shriek towards centre back.*

GRANDMOTHER (*calling*). Daughter! Daughter! Come here! Come here!

MOTHER (*enters hurriedly from the back*). What's the matter? What is it?

GRANDMOTHER (*clutches her and points to the chair*). That? What is that?

MOTHER (*detaches herself and goes gingerly towards the chair*). I'm – not sure. I've never seen one before –

GRANDMOTHER (*shrieks*). Don't go too close! Be careful. Be careful!

MOTHER. It's all right, mother. (*She moves closer.*)

GRANDMOTHER. Oh, the merciful Buddha protect you.

MOTHER (*curious*). I believe I know what it is.

> (*She is very close to it now. The* GRANDMOTHER *is trembling and close to sobbing.*)

GRANDMOTHER. Oh, take care. Take care!

MOTHER (*bending low and peering under the chair*). Yes, I'm sure. It's a chair.

GRANDMOTHER. What is – a – chair? What is it for?

MOTHER. To sit on. I've heard them described.

GRANDMOTHER. To sit on? What kind of beast would seat itself on a hideous thing like that?

MOTHER. Men, mother; men sit on them.

GRANDMOTHER. I don't believe it. Only evil spirits would sit on a devilish device like that.

> (*The* MOTHER *puts out her hand to touch it.*)

Don't touch it. Oh, don't touch it!

MOTHER (*drawing back; a trifle nervously*). It's only made of wood.

GRANDMOTHER. Evil and sorcery reside in wood as well as anything else.

> (*Enter the* FATHER *from right. The* MOTHER *and* GRANDMOTHER *return his bow.*)

FATHER. Did I hear someone shriek? I wasn't properly dressed or I would have come before now to see what the trouble was.

GRANDMOTHER. I shrieked! There are devils in the house, and we are all at the mercy of evil!

FATHER. What's this, my esteemed mother? Devils? Evil?

GRANDMOTHER. There! (*She points an accusing finger at the chair.*)

FATHER. A chair.

MOTHER. I *told* you it was a chair.

FATHER. Where did it come from?

MOTHER. We don't know. It wasn't here a short time ago; I have been in and out putting the bowls on the table.

FATHER (*crosses to it, wonderingly*). A chair. In our house.

MOTHER. You have seen one before, my husband?

FATHER. I have seen them in Tokyo.

MOTHER. Are they made in Tokyo?

FATHER (*laughs*). No, they come from the western countries. The western barbarians sit on them all the time.

GRANDMOTHER. Didn't I say they were from the Devil?

FATHER. Here is how they do it.

> (*He is about to sit in the chair as the* GRANDMOTHER, *as if pursued by seven devils, runs wailing out of the room, centre back.*)

MOTHER. Oh, you have really frightened her now.

FATHER (*seriously*). That was wickedly unfilial of me. I apologize.

(*He bows.*)

MOTHER (*lowering her eyes*). I should not have pointed out that you had.

FATHER. You were quite correct. It is right for you to point out my blunders. You know I have always been liberal in matters such as that.

(*A sound of sobbing is heard, off.*)

MOTHER. I'm afraid your poor mother is crying with fright.

FATHER. I will reassure her. (*Secretly, with mischief.*) But, just before I do, here is how they do it!

(*He lets his seat rest for just a few moments on the chair and then jumps up. But the sight of him even that briefly in this unaccustomed posture is too much for the MOTHER. She bursts into laughter as he crosses to centre, back.*)

MOTHER. You look like a duck.

FATHER (*calling softly*). Mother.

(*The sobbing, off, hesitates, ceases.*)

(*Calls again.*) Mother, your unworthy son is calling you.

GRANDMOTHER (*off*). What is it, my revered son?

FATHER. I send my humble respects to my aged mother and apologize in the dust for frightening her.

GRANDMOTHER. You are – a good son, and I know you wouldn't frighten me purposely.

FATHER. Will you return to us now?

GRANDMOTHER. Are you sitting on – 'It'?

FATHER. No, my mother.

GRANDMOTHER. Are you going to sit on it?

FATHER. No, my mother.

GRANDMOTHER. Are you *touching* it?

FATHER. No.

GRANDMOTHER.   Are you going to touch it?

FATHER.   No.

GRANDMOTHER.   Has it been removed from the room?

FATHER.   No.

GRANDMOTHER.   It is not a good influence in the room. It should be removed.

FATHER.   Do you want me to touch it?

GRANDMOTHER.   No! No! Don't touch it!

FATHER.   Then how am I to remove it, revered mother?

(*The* GRANDMOTHER *appears up-stage.*)

GRANDMOTHER.   If we pray to the Buddha, he will remove it.

FATHER.   I wish I knew how it got here.

MOTHER.   It must *belong* to someone.

FATHER.   But to whom?

(*At this, the* DAUGHTER, *a lovely, proud-looking girl of seventeen, enters quickly from left. She stands facing them.*)

DAUGHTER (*defiantly*).   It is mine!

MOTHER.

FATHER. } Yours!

GRANDMOTHER (*crossing towards her but wary of the chair*). Yours? It was you who brought this sorcerer's instrument into the home of your parents? You who set it down before the shrine of the sacred Buddha?

DAUGHTER (*calmly*).   Yes, it was.

GRANDMOTHER (*stretching out her arms to the Buddha*). Have compassion on the house where evil enters in the hands of its only daughter.

MOTHER.   How could you do such a thing? Aren't you ashamed.

FATHER (*quietly*).   Revered mother, will you please your son by going to your room to prepare for the evening meal?

GRANDMOTHER (*dropping her arms, looking old and weary*). I will go.

(*She moves slowly across and out, right. The* MOTHER *and* FATHER *bow to her.*)

MOTHER. Yes, honoured mother-in-law, go and prepare for your evening meal, and we will take care of this affair.

FATHER. And, my wife, if we are to have supper someone must be in the kitchen to prepare it.

MOTHER. That is so.

(*She bows submissively and exits up-stage.*)
(*The* FATHER *walks to the chair and sits down.*)
(*The* DAUGHTER *stands unmoving in her original position.*)

FATHER. It's not a very comfortable chair, is it?

DAUGHTER. *We* aren't used to sitting in chairs.

FATHER. That is true. Still, I have done so before.

(*The* DAUGHTER *shows interest.*)

In the big cities they are quite commonly seen. But they aren't plain wooden ones like this. Some of them I have seen are made of shining brown cow-hide; cool to the touch and so slippery I would be afraid to sit in one. Others are huge affairs with springs in the seat, and when you sit down it would seem you are sinking into a deep, soft cloud. I imagine the Westerners use them for sleeping. At least the ones I saw seated in them seemed on the verge of sleep.

DAUGHTER. Oh, there are so many things I have *never* seen.

FATHER. That is true of most of us, and many of the things we never see are right before our eyes all the time.

DAUGHTER. I didn't mean *those* things. I mean the new, wonderful things the Westerners have.

FATHER (*rises and takes the chair out, left*). I will put this into the 'shoe-off' room; it disturbs your grandmother.

DAUGHTER. And may I keep it in my room?

FATHER. We will have to think about that.

DAUGHTER. Ishimoto said it was a very fine chair and that houses in America have twenty or thirty each in them.

FATHER (*returns from left*). So it was Ishimoto who gave you the chair? I guessed it was.

DAUGHTER. He didn't give it to me. I bought it.

FATHER. How could you buy it? You have no money.

(*The* FATHER *seats himself on one of the cushions, left.*)

DAUGHTER. I paid him with two of my pearl haircombs, my writing-brush, and the red sash I had at the New Year.

FATHER. And that is how Ishimoto grows richer day by day. Sit here opposite me, and let us talk together as we used to when you were a child.

(*The* DAUGHTER *seats herself on the cushion opposite him.*)

It is here, on this very spot, your old teacher used to teach you your lessons. Don't you remember any longer, with any fondness, all that he told you of our Japanese past, our culture and our wise men, our traditions, and the courageous lives of our history's heroines?

DAUGHTER. I only remember one thing about those lessons, my father.

FATHER. And what is that?

DAUGHTER. That all the two hours my old teacher sat where you sit now and droned into my ear our Japanese past, I was made to sit motionless, so (*she assumes the rigid posture of the Japanese student*); never once was I allowed to move an arm, a hand, or my littlest finger. How the minutes dragged on! I thought he would never finish, that I would turn to stone on the spot and never be able to move again, or run and play in the courtyard.

FATHER. It is true the discipline was harsh —

DAUGHTER. One day, I remember, I felt my left foot grow numb and I ventured to move my trunk the tiniest fraction to relieve the pressure on it. My teacher saw me; he gave me a look like the black God of War. Without a word to me, he stopped the lesson; he got up and left without a bow. I could hear him in the next room complaining loudly to you and saying how unworthy I was. I was left crying with fear and shame.

FATHER. I remember.

DAUGHTER. From that day on, I had my lessons from him in the outer room with no heat, although it was December and the snow was piled high in the streets. I would turn purple with the cold but dared not shiver or tremble in the slightest.

FATHER. Yes, yes. Your mother and I discussed it through an entire night.

DAUGHTER. I didn't know you noticed . . . or cared.

FATHER. We did. We were afraid it would be too hard on you but we decided, in the dawn light, rightly or wrongly, that discipline was the path to wisdom and virtue. We wanted our daughter to be wise and virtuous. We followed custom.

DAUGHTER. Custom!

FATHER. I know you think custom ancient and barbaric.

DAUGHTER. Yes, I do.

FATHER. Yet it is not. It does not diminish men's actions. It gives those actions form. It is our way of respecting others.

DAUGHTER. But it never changes. (*Proudly.*) This is the year nineteen hundred, you know.

FATHER (*amused*). A western year. Nineteen hundred, eh? Did Mr. Ishimoto give you that information? Perhaps free, with the chair?

DAUGHTER (*with child-like mysteriousness*). Oh, I had heard what year it was.

FATHER. Will you believe me if I tell you something?

DAUGHTER. I will try.

FATHER. It is not true that custom fails to change.

DAUGHTER. I don't see that it does.

FATHER. You have not observed it long enough. Do you know there was a day when meat was never eaten in this house? To eat meat was looked upon as a loathsome evil because the

Buddha himself forbade the killing of animals. But gradually the belief began to change. Little by little we were invaded by new ideas from the western world. I well remember the day I first ordered the preparation of meat in this house. My honoured mother spent that day in her room at her personal shrine praying for all of us who dared to break a tradition over a thousand years old. She ate nothing for three days and for two years and more would not eat with us in this room or go near the kitchen where the meat was prepared. To this very hour she has never tasted it and will not if she lives another hundred years.

DAUGHTER.   She is stubborn.

FATHER.   We must all be stubborn in what we believe or one day find we believe in nothing.

DAUGHTER.   But you said you change your beliefs.

FATHER.   I do, and have, and will. When others began to eat meat, I said to myself: Is there some good in this? And I inquired and found there was; that animal flesh makes men stronger and builds muscles to withstand cold and hard work. And so, I said, I will change. We will eat meat in my house. And we did. But not until I had considered it carefully and weighed the custom against the new belief.

DAUGHTER.   Perhaps you have changed – in small things.

FATHER.   Small things?

DAUGHTER.   Eating meat is a small thing to me when I see how chained our lives are.

FATHER.   We are not chained. We are civilized and reserved, it is true –

DAUGHTER.   You call it civilized and reserved, but I call it a prison. I am in prison and I yearn to be free.

> (*Enter* MOTHER *at centre back. She carries a bowl, crosses to the table and places the bowl on it. She putters about as an excuse for eavesdropping.*)

FATHER.   Free to do as you please?

DAUGHTER. Free to do as —

FATHER. As — what?

DAUGHTER. As other women do.

FATHER. What other women?

DAUGHTER. Western women.

FATHER. Ishimoto!

DAUGHTER. Mr. Ishimoto has told me many things; he has painted me a picture of another world — a world I long to know and be a part of. In that world, women are free to grow and blossom instead of sitting with folded hands and allowing life to slip away from them as they do here.

FATHER. Women here live honourable lives.

DAUGHTER (*flatly*). They obey their husbands and bear children and die with never a question on their lips.

FATHER. Is that not honourable?

DAUGHTER. It is not freedom. In the western lands women do not hide behind shutters and sit in an eternal twilight while others regulate their lives.

FATHER. They do not?

DAUGHTER. No. There they walk freely on the streets or go into tea-houses alone and order what they wish and pay for it themselves, for they have their own money.

FATHER. I have heard of that.

DAUGHTER. But, most important, they go to school and learn. They talk to men as their equals and, Mr. Ishimoto says, a wife may even criticize her husband.

> (*The* MOTHER, *who has listened in growing horror, utters an exclamation at this and hurriedly leaves the room.*)

FATHER. My daughter —

DAUGHTER. And it is said that men embrace their wives in front of others and show affection in ways I don't properly understand. But I know it is by more than a bow.

FATHER. It is. I have heard of it. It is called kissing.

DAUGHTER. That's it. That is what Mr. Ishimoto called it.

FATHER. But a kiss is only another custom, strange to us but familiar to them. There is as much feeling of the heart in a bow as there is in a kiss. And yet, to my mind, a bow is in good form because it is an uselfish recognition of another; while a kiss, which is part of love-making, shows a desire for one's own pleasure.

DAUGHTER. It sounds exciting and natural to me.

FATHER. What is natural and what is not? It would seem that all of life must be regulated in some way if we are to live together. One could argue that it is 'natural' to have customs to regulate 'naturalness'.

DAUGHTER (*boldly, then hesitatingly*). I think it is natural for –

FATHER. For what?

DAUGHTER. For a girl to choose her own husband.

FATHER (*rises*). What do you say? Oh, this is too much. I have sat here patiently trying to reason with you, but this is too much.

DAUGHTER. I don't want to marry a man I've never seen.

FATHER. Ungrateful, unfilial child! What do you know, what does any young girl know about choosing a husband? What can she know of his means, his family, his character, his education, which are what matter in a husband?

DAUGHTER. I *won't*! I *won't* marry him.

FATHER. I draw the line. Finally and firmly. Have all the romantic day-dreams you like – no doubt your husband will pay for them – but you *will* marry the man we have chosen for you.

DAUGHTER (*beating her hands on the floor*). No, no, no, no.

FATHER. This is my fault. I should have supervised your education.

DAUGHTER (*sobbing*). Education.

FATHER. But the education of a daughter is always in the hands of the women of the house.

DAUGHTER (*triumphantly*). There, you see? Another *custom!*

(*Enter the* MOTHER, *who brings more bowls to the table. She arranges the cushions and exits right.*)

FATHER. Come. Pick yourself up. Our meal is ready.

(*The* DAUGHTER *rises and wipes her eyes on her sleeve.*)

(*The* FATHER *takes up a position before the gilded shrine.*)

(*Enter* MOTHER *and* GRANDMOTHER *from right. They cross and take up positions behind the* FATHER. *The* DAUGHTER *occupies the final position. At last they are in a row the shape of a semicircle.*)

FATHER. Lord Buddha, Light of Heaven and Earth, giver of Eternal Life, all-wise and merciful, look upon your humble servants and receive their gratitude for your compasionate gift of food.

(*He bows low to the shrine and moves to the right towards the table.*)

(*The* GRANDMOTHER *then bows a deep and reverent bow, going down on her knees to do so. The* MOTHER *bows deeply from the waist. They move away to the right.*)

(*The* DAUGHTER *gives a brief and perfunctory bow and joins the rest.*)

(*They seat themselves at the table, the* FATHER *first in accordance with precedence, and begin their meal. There is silence for several moments.*)

DAUGHTER. Father!

FATHER.

MOTHER.   } Shhhhhhh!

GRANDMOTHER.

(*Silence for a few moments.*)

DAUGHTER (*puts down her bowl, in suppressed emotion*).　I can't —

GRANDMOTHER (*flatly*).　It is not proper to speak at meals.

> (*There is silence again as the* DAUGHTER *fidgets and frets, growing more despairing as the silent moments pass.*)

MOTHER (*in a whisper*).　Don't fidget, daughter. You are disturbing everyone. Calm and tranquillity at mealtime —

DAUGHTER.　Oh, none of you care, none of you care. My heart could be breaking and you would sit there eating silently like cows because it is the custom.

> (*She rises quickly.*)

MOTHER.　Daughter! What are you doing?

GRANDMOTHER.　The sacred Buddha protect us! She has risen from the table.

MOTHER.　Child, child, think what you are doing. No woman rises from her cushion before the master of the household and then only when all are finished. It is an iron rule.

FATHER.　I rise, too. (*Bows to the* GRANDMOTHER *and* MOTHER.) I beg your forgiveness.

> (*They return his bow. He gets up and goes towards the* DAUGHTER.)

Are you completely mad? Have you no respect left at all for your revered mother and your honoured grandmother? Remember, your ideas aren't the only ideas in the world and while you are in your father's house —

DAUGHTER (*interrupting*).　How long will I *be* in it?

GRANDMOTHER }
MOTHER } (*in horror*).　She has interrupted him.

> (*They hide their faces.*)

DAUGHTER.　In a year, a little year, I shall go to some strange house and sit upon the bridal couch with downcast eyes, waiting for a stranger to come and claim me for his slave. I will *not* do it. I will not. I will show you.

(She runs quickly away and out, left.)

FATHER *(turns back to the table and bows again to the two women).* We shall continue our meal. *(He sits and they eat silently.)*

> *(After a few moments there is a sound of sobbing off, left. Those at the table give no indication they hear.)*
>
> *(Enter* DAUGHTER *from left, much transformed and near to hysteria. She has let down her sleek, black hair from its coils and has cut its lengths down to short and jagged lengths. Her gown is covered with hair and she is cutting what lengths remain as she enters.)*

DAUGHTER. There! Now he will not marry me, whoever he is.

> *(The three at the table have, in spite of their control, looked at the* DAUGHTER *and a kind of paralysis has overcome them at the shocking sight. The* FATHER *has half-risen, the* GRANDMOTHER *has hidden her face, the* MOTHER'S *hands are held up as if to ward off a blow.)*

FATHER *(bows hastily to the* MOTHER *and* GRANDMOTHER*).* I must rise.

> *(They bow to him. He rises and faces the* DAUGHTER.*)*

DAUGHTER *(in her sobs).* You see, I meant what I said.

FATHER. You have cut your hair! As a widow would do.

DAUGHTER. Yes, like a widow.

FATHER. This is madness.

DAUGHTER. And if it grows in before my wedding day, I shall pull it out by the roots.

FATHER. Wicked child.

DAUGHTER. No superstitious man would marry me now, looking like a widow, for fear he would die. And they are all superstitious and – stupid.

> *(She exits left. The* GRANDMOTHER *has risen, shaking and trembling, from her cushion. She makes her*

way across the room to the shrine in the desperate,
plodding fashion of a wanderer athirst in the desert
who sights an oasis.)

GRANDMOTHER. I must regain my tranquillity.

(*She kneels before the Buddha and is motionless*
during the following.)

MOTHER (*still seated*). My husband!

FATHER. Yes.

MOTHER. Is this — my fault? Some fault of mine?

FATHER. No, it is mine. How could you know of all the
new ideas abroad in our country or how they might change
your daughter from day to day, tearing her from the old ways?

MOTHER. If she does not marry him, there will be great
shame on our family name.

FATHER. It will be remembered from generation to generation.

MOTHER. Could she not be forced to marry him?

FATHER. She could be.

(*The* GRANDMOTHER *rises and comes to them.*)

GRANDMOTHER. She is not a child to be forced. She would
only grow more rebellious and by her unwifely actions bring
shame to our good name after her marriage.

MOTHER. What are we to do?

GRANDMOTHER (*despairingly*). Oh, the old, safe ways are
crumbling. In my day tradition and discipline gave women
strength in their duty and joy in their lives. But now, the
scourge has spread across the land, destroying the ancient virtues of humility and modesty. Have you not seen, even here,
how some women hurry along the paths at an unseemly rate
until they are walking like men?

MOTHER. I have seen that.

GRANDMOTHER. They no longer arrange flowers in the
classical manner but place them in the vase as if they were
growing in natural chaos.

FATHER. It is so.

GRANDMOTHER. They neglect to subdue their voices when they speak and fail to bow to their elders at the proper times – oh, it is all around us – all around us – and now it has struck our home.

FATHER. It is my fault. Not to have protected her from these influences was a great fault in me.

⸱ GRANDMOTHER. Forgive my rude contradiction, but the fault is ours.

MOTHER. Yes, it is ours. In our hands she was moulded.

GRANDMOTHER. More particularly, the fault is mine. As the eldest, it was my duty to conserve in her the traditions of my life and the order of my discipline.

FATHER. Don't blame yourselves. I do not blame you. The forces from without, which have come like hurricanes from across the sea, are powerful. Hardly a home has not felt them.

GRANDMOTHER. We are as powerful as they. We understand how to sacrifice to save all we hold precious. As in the past, sacrifices were made – as in the past.

FATHER. My revered mother –

GRANDMOTHER. Does the child love me?

MOTHER. There is no doubt of that. Ever since she was a child and you brought her pears from the orchard, carved her pumpkin at the Harvest Festival, and presented her with her new year's sash, she has loved you.

GRANDMOTHER. Then, since it is so, there is some respect, too? Somewhere, deep in her heart?

MOTHER. Oh, there is. She is not a wicked child. Only headstrong and easily swayed by something new. This will pass. I pray it will pass and she will be a helpmate to her husband and win respect at the shrines of her ancestors.

GRANDMOTHER. It may pass. But not unless my generation sets an example.

FATHER. Sets an example, my mother?

GRANDMOTHER. That is what we have failed to do. We have been self-indulgent and complacent, thinking our ways safe against time and influence. We have failed to renew the old faith, have failed to sacrifice everything for our beliefs to show how greatly the heart may be swayed by duty. We have lost courage.

FATHER. My mother —

GRANDMOTHER. You know my meaning. It is the ancient, accepted way. It is the only way I know to right a wrong in the eyes of the gods and in the eyes of our watchful forebears. Otherwise, I am helpless and can make no protest except with the cawing tongue of an old woman, which no one heeds.

     (*She rises and moves slowly towards exit, right, as the*
        MOTHER *and* FATHER *bow low in profound respect.*)

FATHER. We will worship at your shrine, noble mother.

GRANDMOTHER. I thank you, my son. I will keep my watch over you.

     (*She bows and exits.*)

FATHER. Bring our daughter here.

     (*The* MOTHER *bows and exits, left.*)

     (*The* FATHER *stands, looking at the shrine intently as*
       if trying to read the secret of life in the calm and
       gracious features of the timeless Buddha.)

     (*Enter* DAUGHTER *and* MOTHER *from left. The* MOTHER
       goes to the shrine, kneels before the Buddha and
       remains immobile during the following.)

FATHER (*gently*). My daughter, your hair was beautiful a few short minutes ago.

DAUGHTER (*subdued and exhausted*). Yes.

FATHER. Do you recall, as a child, how mortified you were when the ends of your hair would curl instead of hanging straight like other little girls'?

DAUGHTER. I remember.

FATHER. Do you remember, as well, who it was who studied in old books, who made up the sticky solution, and who bought a special stiff brush with her rice-cake money? Who sat patiently hour upon hour, combing and brushing and combing again, and brushing a thousand times over, so that your hair would be straight?

DAUGHTER. It was grandmother.

FATHER. And do you know why she did that?

DAUGHTER. To make my hair straight.

FATHER. More than that. It was to save you from shame. To set you an example of sacrifice and duty. She knew that if your hair was not straight your family would be ridiculed as well as you. And it is a woman's duty to save the honour of her family however she can. In small matters – and in great.

DAUGHTER. I can't help it if I don't think the way everyone else does.

FATHER. Honour is the same for us all.

DAUGHTER. Honour – ?

FATHER. It is a word you have heard many times. Have you understood what it meant?

DAUGHTER (*petulantly*). Oh, I don't know.

FATHER. Honour is the high reputation which we deserve, not by always being right, but by always living with respect and in accord with true principles.

DAUGHTER. How do you know when a principle is true?

FATHER. Perhaps you must look into the deeps of your heart to see how full its meaning is.

> (*There is a noise off, right, as of an instrument falling to the floor.*)
>
> (*The* MOTHER *rises unobtrusively from the shrine and exits, centre back.*)

DAUGHTER. I believe all I have said.

FATHER. Do you believe in it strongly?

DAUGHTER. Yes, I do.

FATHER. With courage?

DAUGHTER. Yes.

FATHER. Enough to sacrifice for it?

DAUGHTER. Yes.

FATHER. Enough to sacrifice – supremely?

(*The* MOTHER *appears at right. She bows low.*)

MOTHER. My honoured husband, your revered mother is now with her ancestors.

(*She kneels in prayer, facing the inner room, right.*)

DAUGHTER (*staggered*). My grandmother – ? My grandmother – ?

FATHER. Yes.

DAUGHTER. Gone – to the other world?

FATHER. It was by her own choice and by her own hand.

DAUGHTER. Father – why? Oh, father, why?

FATHER. Because she believed and had no other protest against your disbelief.

DAUGHTER (*going slowly, as if hypnotized, towards exit, right*). Against – my – disbelief – ?

FATHER. Yes, go in to her, so that sacrifice and honour will no longer be only words to you.

(*The* DAUGHTER *exits right.*)

(*The* FATHER *goes to the shrine and kneels before it.*)

(*After a few moments, the* DAUGHTER *enters from right, in the extreme agitation of her horror.*)

DAUGHTER. Mother! Mother!

(*The* MOTHER *does not move. The* DAUGHTER *runs across to the* FATHER.)

My father! My father!

(*He does not move. She turns and comes down-stage.*)

I believe – I believe –

(*She falls down onto a cushion.*)

(*In a wail of anguish.*) Oh, I don't know what I believe.
    (*She is sobbing and beating her hands, as the curtain falls.*)

A CHILD IS BORN

by

STEPHEN VINCENT BENÉT

CHARACTERS

Narrator
The Innkeeper of Bethlehem
The Innkeeper's Wife
Roman soldier
Sarah
Leah
Servants at the inn
St. Joseph
The Blessed Virgin Mary (represented by music
    only)
Three Shepherds
Kings from the East
Dismas, a thief

(Music, as broadcast opens. It fades. NARRATOR *speaks.)*
   NARRATOR.   I'm your narrator. It's my task to say
Just where and how things happen in our play,
Set the bare stage with words instead of props
And keep on talking till the curtain drops.
So you shall know, as well as our poor skill
Can show you, whether it is warm or chill,
Indoors or out, a battle or a fair,
In this, our viewless theatre of the air.
It's an old task – old as the human heart,
Old as those bygone players and their art
Who, in old days when faith was nearer earth,
Played out the mystery of Jesus' birth
In hall or village green or market square
For all who chose to come and see them there,
And, if they knew that King Herod, in his crown,
Was really Wat, the cobbler of the town,
And Tom, the fool, played Abraham the Wise,
They did not care. They saw with other eyes.
The story was their own – not far away,
As real as if it happened yesterday,
Full of all awe and wonder yet so near,
A marvellous thing that could have happened here
In their own town – a star that could have blazed
On their own shepherds, leaving them amazed,
Frightened and questioning and following still
To the bare stable – and the miracle.

So we, tonight, who are your players too,
Ask but to tell that selfsame tale to you
In our own words, the plain and simple speech

Of human beings, talking each to each,
Troubled with their own cares, not always wise,
And yet, at moments, looking towards the skies.

The time is — time. The place is anywhere.
The voices speak to you across the air
To say that once again a child is born.
A child is born.
'I pray you all, give us your audience
And hear this matter with reverence.'
          (*Music.*)
There is a town where men and women live
Their lives as people do in troubled times,
Times when the world is shaken. There is an inn.
A woman sings there in the early morning.
          (*Music, fading into the voice of a woman — the* INN-
              KEEPER'S WIFE *— singing as she goes about her
              household tasks.*)
     INNKEEPER'S WIFE.   In Bethlehem of Judea
There shall be born a child,
A child born of woman
And yet undefiled.

He shall not come to riches,
To riches and might,
But in the bare stable
He shall be Man's light.

He shall not come to conquest,
The conquest of kings,
But in the bare stable
He shall judge all things.

King Herod, King Herod,
Now what will you say

Of the child in the stable
This cold winter day?

I hear the wind blowing
Across the bare thorn,
I fear not King Herod
If this child may be born.

>(*Sound of steps coming down a flight of stone stairs.
A man's voice, rough and suspicious – the voice of
the* INNKEEPER. *The innkeeper is middle-aged – his
wife somewhat younger.*)

INNKEEPER. Singing again! I told you not to sing!

WIFE. I'm sorry. I forgot.

INNKEEPER. Forgot? That's fine!
That's wonderful! That answers everything!
The times are hard enough and bad enough
For anyone who tries to keep an inn,
Get enough bread to stick in his own mouth
And keep things going, somehow, in his town.
The country's occupied. We have no country.
You've heard of that, perhaps?
You've seen their soldiers, haven't you? You know
Just what can happen to our sort of people
Once there's a little trouble? Answer me!

WIFE (*wearily*). I've seen. I know.

INNKEEPER. You've seen. You know. And you keep singing
songs!
Not ordinary songs – the kind of songs
That might bring in a little bit of trade,
Songs with a kind of pleasant wink in them
That make full men forget the price of the wine,
The kind of songs a handsome girl can sing
After their dinner to good customers
– And, thanks to me, the inn still has a few! –

Oh, no! You have to sing rebellious songs
About King Herod!

    WIFE.   I'm sorry. I forgot.

    INNKEEPER.   Sorry? Forgot? You're always saying that!
Is it your business what King Herod does?
Is it your place to sing against King Herod?

    WIFE.   I think that he must be a wicked man.
A very wicked man.

    INNKEEPER.   Oh, la, la, la!
Sometimes *I* think your ways will drive me mad.
Are you a statesman or a general?
Do you pretend to know the ins and outs
Of politics and why the great folk do
The things they do – and why we have to bear them?
Because it's we – we – we
Who have to bear them, first and last and always,
In every country and in every time.
They grind us like dry wheat between the stones.
Don't you know that?

    WIFE.   I know that, somehow, kings
Should not be wicked and grind down the people.
I know that kings like Herod should not be.

    INNKEEPER.   All right – all right. I'm not denying that.
I'm reasonable enough. I know the world.
I'm willing to admit to anyone
At least behind closed doors
        (*He drops his voice.*)
That Herod isn't quite my sort of king
And that I don't approve of all he does.
Still, there he is. He's king. How will it help
If I go out and write on someone's wall
        (*In a whisper.*)
'Down with King Herod!'
        (*His voice comes up again.*)

What's it worth?
The cross for me, the whipping-post for you,
The inn burned down, the village fined for treason,
Just because one man didn't like King Herod.
For that's the way things are.

    WIFE. Yet there are men —

    INNKEEPER. Oh, yes, I know — fanatics, rabble, fools,
Outcasts of war, misfits, rebellious souls,
Seekers of some vague kingdom in the stars —
They hide out in the hills and stir up trouble,
Call themselves prophets, too, and prophesy
That something new is coming to the world,
The Lord knows what!
Well, it's a long time coming,
And, meanwhile, we're the wheat between the stones.

    WIFE. Something must come.

    INNKEEPER. Believe it if you choose,
But, meantime, if we're clever, we can live
And even thrive a little — clever wheat
That slips between the grinding stones and grows
In little green blade-sprinkles on the ground.
At least, if you'll not sing subversive songs
To other people but your poor old husband.

        (*Changing tone.*)
Come, wife, I've got some news.
I didn't mean to be so angry with you.
You've some queer fancies in that head of yours
  Lord, don't I know! — but you're still the tall girl
With the grave eyes and the brook-running voice
I took without a dower or a price
Out of your father's house because — oh, well —
Because you came. And they've not been so bad,
The years since then. Now have they?

    WIFE. No.

INNKEEPER.   That's right.
Give us a kiss.
    (*Pause.*)
    I couldn't help the child.
I know you think of that, this time of year.
He was my son, too, and I think of him.
I couldn't help his dying.
    WIFE.   No, my husband.
    INNKEEPER.   He stretched his little arms to me and died.
And yet I had the priest — the high priest, too.
I didn't spare the money.
    WIFE.   No, my husband.
I am a barren bough. I think and sing
And am a barren bough.
    INNKEEPER.   Oh, come, come, come!
    WIFE.   The fault is mine. I had my joyous season,
My season of full ripening and fruit
And then the silence and the aching breast.
I thought I would have children. I was wrong,
But my flesh aches to think I do not have them.
I did not mean to speak of this at all.
I do not speak of it. I will be good.
There is much left — so much.
The kindness and the bond that lasts the years
And all the small and treasurable things
That make up life and living. Do not care
So much. I have forgotten. I'll sing softly,
Not sing at all. It was long past and gone.
Tell me your news. Is it good news?
    INNKEEPER (*eagerly*).   The best!
The prefect comes to dinner here tonight
With all his officers — oh yes, I know,
The enemy — of course, the enemy —
But someone has to feed them.

WIFE. And they'll pay?

INNKEEPER. Cash.

WIFE. On the nail?

INNKEEPER. Yes.

WIFE. Good.

INNKEEPER. I thought you'd say so.
Oh, we'll make no great profit — not tonight —
I've seen the bill of fare they asked of me,
Quails, in midwinter! Well, we'll give them — quails!
And charge them for them, too! You know the trick?

WIFE. Yes.

INNKEEPER. They must be well served. I'll care for that,
The honest innkeeper, the thoughtful man,
Asking, 'Your worship, pray another glass
Of our poor wine! Your worship, is the roast
Done to your worship's taste? Oh, nay, nay, nay,
Your worship, all was settled in the bill,
So do not spoil my servants with largesse,
Your worship!' — And he won't. He pinches pennies.
But, once he's come here, he will come again,
And we shall live, not die, and put some coin,
Some solid, enemy and lovely coin
Under the hearthstone, eh?
Spoil the Egyptians, eh?
          (*He laughs.*)
That's my war and my battle and my faith.
The war of every sane and solid man
And, even if we have no child to follow us,
It shall be won, I tell you!
          (*There is a knock at the outer door.*)
Hark! What's that?
I'll go — the maids aren't up yet — lazybones!
          (*The knock is repeated, imperatively.*)
INNKEEPER (*grumbling*). A minute — just a minute!

It's early yet — you needn't beat the door down.
This is an honest inn.

(*He shoots the bolts and opens the door, while speaking.*)
Good morning.

SOLDIER'S VOICE.   Hail Caesar! Are you the keeper of this inn?

INNKEEPER.   Yes, sir.

SOLDIER.   Orders from the prefect. No other guests shall be entertained at your inn tonight after sundown. The prefect wishes all the rooms to be at the disposal of his guests.

INNKEEPER.   All the rooms?

SOLDIER.   You understand plain Latin, don't you?

INNKEEPER.   Yes, sir, but —

SOLDIER.   Well?

INNKEEPER.   Sir, when the prefect first commanded me,
There was a party of my countrymen
Engaged for a small room — he'd hear no noise —
No noise at all —

SOLDIER.   This is the prefect's feast — the Saturnalia —
You've heard your orders.

INNKEEPER.   Yes, sir. Yes, indeed, sir.

SOLDIER.   See they are carried out! No other guests! Hail Caesar!

INNKEEPER (*feebly*).   Hail Caesar!
(*He slams the door.*)
Well, that's pleasant.
All the rooms at the disposal of the prefect!
No other guests! I'll have to warn Ben Ezra.
But he's a sound man — he will understand.
We'll cook his mutton here and send it to him.
And the wine, too — a bottle of good wine —
The second best and let the prefect pay for it!
That will make up. No other guests. Remember
No other guests!

WIFE.   I will remember.

INNKEEPER. Do so.
It is an order. Now, about the quail.
You'll make the sauce. That's the important thing.
A crow can taste like a quail, with a good sauce.
You have your herbs?

WIFE. Yes.

INNKEEPER. Well then, begin, begin!
It's morning and we haven't too much time
And the day's bitter cold. Well, all the better.
They'll drink the more but — all this work to do
And the fire barely started! Sarah! Leah!
Where are those lazy servants? Where's the fish?
Where's the new bread? Why haven't we begun?
Leah and Sarah, come and help your mistress!
I'll rouse the fools! There's work to do today!

> (*He stamps up the stairs. She moves about her business.*)

WIFE (*singing*). In Bethlehem of Judea
There was an inn also.
There was no room within it.
For any but the foe.

No child might be born there.
No bud come to bloom.
For there was no chamber
And there was no room.

> (*Her voice fades off into music which swells up and down.*)

NARRATOR. And the day passed and night fell on the town,
Silent and still and cold. The houses lay
Huddled and dark beneath the watching stars
And only the inn windows streamed with light —

> (*Fade into offstage noise of a big party going on upstairs.*)

1ST VOICE (*offstage*).   Ha, ha, ha! And then the Cilician said to the Ethiopian. He said —

2ND VOICE (*offstage*).   Well, I remember when we first took Macedonia. There was a girl there —

3RD VOICE (*offstage*).   Quiet, gentlemen, quiet — the prefect wishes to say a few words —

PREFECT'S VOICE (*off*).   Gentlemen — men of Rome — mindful of Rome's historic destiny — and of our good friend King Herod — who has chosen alliance with Rome rather than a useless struggle — keep them under with a firm hand —

SARAH.   What is he saying up there?

LEAH.   I don't know.
I don't know the big words. The soldier said —

SARAH.   You and your soldier!

LEAH.   Oh, he's not so bad.
He brought me a trinket — see!

SARAH.   You and your Roman trinkets! I hate serving them. I'd like to spit in their cups each time I serve them.

LEAH.   You wouldn't dare!

SARAH.   Wouldn't I, though?
    (*There are steps on the stairs as the* INNKEEPER *comes down.*)

INNKEEPER.   Here, here.
What's this, what's this, why are you standing idle?
They're calling for more wine!

SARAH.   Let Leah serve them.
She likes their looks!

WIFE.   Sarah!

SARAH (*sighs*).   Yes, mistress.

WIFE.   Please, Sarah — we've talked like this so many times.

SARAH.   Very well, mistress. But let her go first.
    (*To* LEAH.)
Get up the stairs, you little soldier's comfort!
I hope he pinches you!

LEAH. Mistress, it's not my fault. Does Sarah have to —
WIFE. Oh, go, go — both of you!
    (*They mutter and go upstairs.*)
INNKEEPER. Well, that's a pretty little tempest for you.
You ought to beat the girl. She's insolent.
And shows it.
  WIFE. We can't be too hard on her.
Her father's dead, her brother's in the hills,
And yet she used to be a merry child.
I can remember her when she was merry,
A long time since.
  INNKEEPER. You always take their side
And yet, you'd think a self-respecting inn
Could have some decent and well-mannered maids!
But no such luck — sullen and sluts, the lot of them!
Give me a stool — I'm tired.
      (*He sits, muttering.*)
Say thirty dinners
And double for the prefect — and the wine —
Best, second best and common — h'm, not bad
But then —
      (*Suddenly.*)
Why do you sit there, staring at the fire,
So silent and so waiting and so still?
      (*Unearthly music, very faint at first, begins with the
        next speech and builds through the scene.*)
  WIFE. I do not know. I'm waiting.
  INNKEEPER. Waiting for what?
  WIFE. I do not know. For something new and strange,
Something I've dreamt about in some deep sleep,
Truer than any waking,
Heard about, long ago, so long ago,
In sunshine and the summer grass of childhood,
When the sky seems so near.

I do not know its shape, its will, its purpose
And yet all day its will has been upon me,
More real than any voice I ever heard,
More real than yours or mine or our dead child's,
More real than all the voices there upstairs,
Brawling above their cups, more real than light.
And there is light in it and fire and peace,
Newness of heart and strangeness like a sword,
And all my body trembles under it,
And yet I do not know.

INNKEEPER.　You're tired, my dear.
Well, we shall sleep soon.

WIFE.　No, I am not tired.
I am expectant as a runner is
Before a race, a child before a feast day,
A woman at the gates of life and death,
Expectant for us all, for all of us
Who live and suffer on this little earth
With such small brotherhood. Something begins.
Something is full of change and sparkling stars.
Something is loosed that changes all the world.

　　　　(*Music up and down.*)

And yet — I cannot read it yet. I wait
And strive — and cannot find it.

　　　　(*A knock at the door.*)

Hark? What's that?

INNKEEPER.　They can't come in. I don't care who they are.
We have no room.

　　　　(*Knock is repeated.*)

WIFE.　Go to the door!

　　　　(*He goes and opens the door.*)

INNKEEPER.　Well?

　　　　(*Strain of music.*)

JOSEPH (*from outside*).   Is this the inn? Sir, we are travellers
And it is late and cold. May we enter?
  WIFE (*eagerly*).   Who is it?
  INNKEEPER (*to her*).   Just a pair of country people,
A woman and a man. I'm sorry for them
But —
  JOSEPH.   My wife and I are weary,
May we come in?
  INNKEEPER.   I'm sorry, my good man.
We have no room tonight. The prefect's orders.
  JOSEPH.   No room at all?
  INNKEEPER.   Now, now, it's not my fault.
You look like honest and well-meaning folk
And nobody likes turning trade away
But I'm not my own master. Not tonight.
It may be, in the morning —
        (*He starts to close the door.*)
  WIFE.   Wait!
  INNKEEPER (*in a fierce whisper*).   Must you mix in this?
  WIFE.   Wait!
        (*She goes to the door.*)
Good sir, the enemy are in our house
And we —
        (*She sees the* VIRGIN, *who does not speak throughout
          this scene but is represented by music.*)
  WIFE.   Oh.
        (*Music.*)
  WIFE (*haltingly*).   I — did not see your wife. I did not know.
  JOSEPH (*simply*).   Her name is Mary. She is near her time.
  WIFE.   Yes. Yes.
        (*To the* INNKEEPER.)
Go — get a lantern.
Quickly!
  INNKEEPER.   What?

WIFE. *Quickly!*
          (*To* JOSEPH *and* MARY.)
I — I once had a child.
We have no room. That's true.
And it would not be right. Not here. Not now.
Not with those men whose voices you can hear,
Voices of death and iron — King Herod's voices.
Better the friendly beasts. What am I saying?
There is — we have a stable at the inn,
Safe from the cold, at least — and, if you choose,
You shall be very welcome. It is poor
But the poor share the poor their crumbs of bread
Out of God's hand, so gladly,
And that may count for something. Will you share it?
     JOSEPH. Gladly and with great joy.
     WIFE. The lantern, husband!
     JOSEPH. Nay, I will take it. I can see the path. Come!
          (*Music up.* JOSEPH *and* MARY *go.* INNKEEPER *and* WIFE
          watch them.)
     INNKEEPER (*to wife*). Well, I suppose that you must have
          your way
And, any other night — They're decent people
Or seem to be —
     WIFE. He has his arm about her, smoothing out
The roughness of the path for her.
     INNKEEPER. — Although
They are not even people of our town,
As I suppose you know —
     WIFE. So rough a path to tread with weary feet!
     INNKEEPER. Come in.
          (*He shivers.*)
Brr, there's a frost upon the air tonight.
I'm cold or — yes, I must be cold. That's it.
That's it, now, to be sure. Come, shut the door.

WIFE.   Something begins, begins;
Starlit and sunlit, something walks abroad
In flesh and spirit and fire.
Something is loosed to change the shaken world.
(Music up and down. A bell strikes the hour.)
NARRATOR.   The night deepens. The stars march in the sky.
The prefect's men are gone. The inn is quiet
Save for the sleepy servants and their mistress,
Who clean the last soiled pots.
The innkeeper drowses before the fire.
But, in the street, outside —
(Music, changing into a shepherd's carol.)
1ST SHEPHERD.   As we poor shepherds watched by night
CHORUS.   With a hey, with a ho.
1ST SHEPHERD.   A star shone over us so bright
We left our flocks to seek its light
CHORUS.   In excelsis Deo,
Gloria, gloria,
In excelsis Deo.
1ST SHEPHERD.   We left our silly sheep to stray,
CHORUS.   With a hey, with a ho.
1ST SHEPHERD.   They'll think us no good shepherds, they.
And yet we came a blessed way
CHORUS.   In excelsis Deo,
Gloria, gloria,
In excelsis Deo.
1ST SHEPHERD.   Now how may such a matter be?
CHORUS.   With a hey, with a ho.
1ST SHEPHERD.   That we of earth, poor shepherds we,
May look on Jesu's majesty?
And yet the star says — 'It is He!'
2ND SHEPHERD.   It is He!
3RD SHEPHERD.   It is He!
CHORUS.   Sing excelsis Deo,

Gloria, gloria,
In excelsis Deo!

SARAH. Who sings so late? How can they sing so late?

LEAH. I'll go and see.
Wait – I'll rub the windowpane.
It's rimed with frost.
(*She looks out.*)
They're shepherds from the hills.

WIFE. Shepherds?

LEAH. Yes, mistress. They have crooks and staves.
Their tattered cloaks are ragged on their backs.
Their hands are blue and stinging with the cold
And yet they all seem drunken, not with wine
But with good news. Their faces shine with it.

WIFE. Cold – and so late. Poor creatures – call them in.
The prefect's men are gone.

LEAH. Aye but – the master –

WIFE. He's dozing. Do as I tell you.

LEAH (*calling out*). Come in – come in – tarry awhile and rest!

SHEPHERDS (*joyously*). We cannot stay. We follow the bright star.

Gloria, gloria,
In excelsis Deo!

WIFE. Where did they go? Would they not stay with us? Not one?

LEAH. Mistress, they did not even look on me.
They looked ahead. They have gone towards the stable,
The stable of our inn.

LEAH (*excitedly*). Aye – gone but – Mistress! Mistress! Do you hear?

WIFE. Hear what?

LEAH. The tread of steeds on the hard ground,
Iron-hoofed, ringing clear – a company

That comes from out the East. I've never seen
Such things. I am afraid. These are great lords,
Great kings, with strange and memorable beasts,
And crowns upon their heads!

INNKEEPER (*waking*).   What's that? What's that?
Lords, nobles, kings, here in Bethlehem,
In our poor town? What fortune! Oh, what fortune!
Stand from the window there, you silly girl,
I'll speak to them!

> (*He calls out.*)

My gracious noble masters,
Worthy and mighty kings! Our humble inn
Is honoured by your high nobility!
Come in — come in — we've fire and beds and wine!
Come in — come in — tarry awhile and rest!

KINGS' VOICES (*joyfully*).   We cannot stay! We follow the
bright star!
Gloria, gloria,
In excelsis Deo!

INNKEEPER.   I do not understand it. They are gone.
They did not even look at me or pause
Though there's no other inn.
They follow the poor shepherds to the stable.

WIFE.   They would not tarry with us — no, not one.

INNKEEPER.   And yet —

WIFE.   Peace, husband. You know well enough.
Why none would tarry with us.
And so do I. I lay awhile in sleep
And a voice said to me, 'Gloria, gloria,
Gloria in excelsis Deo.
The child is born, the child, the child is born!'
And yet I did not rise and go to him,
Though I had waited and expected long,
For I was jealous that my child should die

And her child live,
And so – I have my judgment. And it is just.

INNKEEPER.   Dreams.

WIFE.   Were they dreams, the shepherds and the kings?
Is it a dream, this glory that we feel
Streaming upon us – and yet not for us.

LEAH.   Now, mistress, mistress, 'tis my fault not yours.
You told me to seek the strangers in the stable
And see they had all care but I – forgot.

SARAH.   Kissing your soldier!

LEAH.   Sarah!

SARAH.   I am sorry, Leah.
My tongue's too sharp. Mistress, the fault was mine.
You told me also and I well remembered
Yet did not go.

WIFE.   Sarah.

SARAH.   I did not go.
Brooding on mine own wrongs, I did not go.
It was my fault.

INNKEEPER.   If there was any fault, wife, it was mine.
I did not wish to turn them from my door
And yet – I know I love the chink of money,
Love it too well, the good, sound, thumping coin,
Love it – oh, God, since I am speaking truth,
Better than wife or fire or chick or child,
Better than country, better than good fame,
Would sell my people for it in the street,
Oh, for a price – but sell them.
And there are many like me. And God pity us.

WIFE.   God pity us indeed, for we are human,
And do not always see
The vision when it comes, the shining change,
Or, if we see it, do not follow it,
Because it is too hard, too strange, too new,

Too unbelievable, too difficult,
Warring too much with common, easy ways,
And now I know this, standing in this light,
Who have been half alive these many years,
Brooding on my own sorrow, my own pain,
Saying 'I am a barren bough. Expect
Nor fruit nor blossom from a barren bough.'
Life is not lost by dying! Life is lost
Minute by minute, day by dragging day,
In all the thousand, small, uncaring ways,
The smooth appeasing compromises of time,
Which are King Herod and King Herod's men,
Always and always. Life can be
Lost without vision but not lost by death,
Lost by not caring, willing, going on
Beyond the ragged edge of fortitude
To something more – something no man has seen.
You who love money, you who love yourself,
You who love bitterness, and I, who loved
And lost and thought I could not love again,
And all the people of this little town,
Rise up! The loves we had were not enough.
Something is loosed to change the shaken world,
And with it we must change!

>   (*The voice of* DISMAS, *the thief, breaking in – a rather*
>   *quizzical, independent voice.*)

DISMAS.   Now that's well said!

INNKEEPER.   Who speaks there? Who are you?

DISMAS.   Who? Oh, my name is Dismas. I'm a thief.
You know the starved, flea-bitten sort of boy
Who haunts dark alleyways in any town,
Sleeps on a fruit sack, runs from the police,
Begs what he can and – borrows what he must.
That's me!

INNKEEPER.   How did you get here?

DISMAS.   By the door, innkeeper,
The cellar door. The lock upon it's old.
I could pick locks like that when I was five.

INNKEEPER.   What have you taken?

DISMAS.   Nothing.
I tried the stable first — and then your cellar,
Slipped in, crept up, rolled underneath a bench,
While all your honest backs were turned — and then —

WIFE.   And then?

DISMAS.   Well — something happened. I don't know what.
I didn't see your shepherds or your kings,
But, in the stable, I did see the child,
Just through a crack in the boards — one moment's space.
That's all that I can tell you.
        (*Passionately.*)
Is he for me as well? Is he for me?

WIFE.   For you as well.

DISMAS.   Is he for all of us?
There are so many of us, worthy mistress,
Beggars who show their sores and ask for alms,
Women who cough their lungs out in the cold,
Slaves — oh, I've been one! — thieves and runagates
Who knife each other for a bite of bread,
— The vast sea of the wretched and the poor,
Whose murmur comes so faintly to your ears
In this fine country.
Has he come to all of us
Or just to you?

WIFE.   To every man alive.

DISMAS.   I wish I could believe.

SARAH (*scornfully*).   And, if you did,
No doubt you'd give up thieving!

DISMAS.   Gently, lady, gently.

Thieving's my trade — the only trade I know.
But, if it were true,
If he had really come to all of us —
I say, to all of us —
Then, honest man or thief,
I'd hang upon a cross for him!
              (*A shocked pause. The others mutter.*)
    DISMAS.   Would you?
              (*Another pause.*)
I see that I've said something you don't like,
Something uncouth and bold and terrifying,
And yet, I'll tell you this:
It won't be till each one of us is willing,
Not you, not me, but every one of us,
To hang upon a cross for every man
Who suffers, starves and dies,
Fight his sore battles as they were our own,
And help him from the darkness and the mire,
That there will be no crosses and no tyrants,
No Herods and no slaves.
              (*Another pause.*)
Well, it was pleasant, thinking things might be so.
And so I'll say farewell. I've taken nothing.
And he was a fair child to look on.
    WIFE.   Wait!
    DISMAS.   Why? What is it you see there, by the window?
    WIFE.   The dawn, the common day,
The ordinary, poor and mortal day.
The shepherds and the kings have gone away.
The great angelic visitors are gone.
He is alone. He must not be alone.
    INNKEEPER.   I do not understand you, wife.
    DISMAS.   Nor I.
    WIFE.   Do you not see, because I see at last?

Dismas, the thief, is right.
He comes to all of us or comes to none.
Not to my heart in joyous recompense
For what I lost — not to your heart or yours,
But to the ignorant heart of all the world,
So slow to alter, so confused with pain.
Do you not see he must not be alone?

INNKEEPER.   I think that I begin to see. And yet —

WIFE.   We are the earth his word must sow like wheat
And, if it finds no earth, it cannot grow.
We are his earth, the mortal and the dying,
Led by no star — the sullen and the slut,
The thief, the selfish man, the barren woman,
Who have betrayed him once and will betray him,
Forget his words, be great a moment's space
Under the strokes of chance,
And then sink back into our small affairs.
And yet, unless *we* go, his message fails.

LEAH.   Will he bring peace, will he bring brotherhood?

WIFE.   He would bring peace, he would bring brotherhood
And yet he will be mocked at in the street.

SARAH.   Will he slay King Herod
And rule us all?

WIFE.   He will not slay King Herod. He will die.
There will be other Herods, other tyrants,
Great wars and ceaseless struggles to be free,
Not always won.

INNKEEPER.   These are sad tidings of him.

WIFE.   No, no — they are glad tidings of great joy,
Because he brings man's freedom in his hands,
Not as a coin that may be spent or lost
But as a living fire within the heart,
Never quite quenched — because he brings to all,
The thought, the wish, the dream of brotherhood,

Never and never to be wholly lost,
The water and the bread of the oppressed,
The stay and succour of the resolute,
The harness of the valiant and the brave,
The new word that has changed the shaken world.
And, though he die, his word shall grow like wheat
And every time a child is born,
In pain and love and freedom hardly won,
Born and gone forth to help and aid mankind,
There will be women with a right to say
'Gloria, gloria in excelsis Deo!
A child is born!'

SARAH.   Gloria!

LEAH.   Gloria!

WIFE.   Come, let us go. What can we bring to him?
What mortal gifts?

LEAH (*shyly*).   I have a ribbon. It's my prettiest.
It is not much but – he might play with it.

SARAH.   I have a little bell my father gave me.
It used to make me merry. I have kept it.
I – he may have it.

DISMAS.   My pocket's empty and my rags are bare.
But I can sing to him. That's what I'll do
And – if he needs a thief to die for him –

INNKEEPER.   I would give all my gold.
I will give my heart.

WIFE.   And I my faith through all the years and years,
Though I forget, though I am led astray,
Though, after this I never see his face,
I will give all my faith.
Come, let us go,
We, the poor earth but we, the faithful earth,
Not yet the joyful, not yet the triumphant,
But faithful, faithful, through the mortal years!

Come!
> (*Music begins.*)

DISMAS (*sings*).   Come, all ye faithful.

INNKEEPER.   Joyful and triumphant.

WOMEN.   Come ye, O come ye to Bethlehem!
> (*Their voices rise in chorus in 'Come, all ye faithful.'
> The chorus and the music swell.*)

CURTAIN

THE RING OF GENERAL MACÍAS

A drama of the Mexican Revolution

by

JOSEPHINA NIGGLI

CHARACTERS

Marica, the sister of General Macías
Raquel, the wife of General Macías
Andres de la O, a captain in the Revolutionary
    Army
Cleto, a private in the Revolutionary Army
Basilio Flores, a captain in the Federal Army

PLACE: Just outside Mexico City

TIME: A Night in April, 1912

SCENE: *The living-room of General Macías' home is luxuriously furnished in the gold and ornate style of Louis XVI. In the right wall are french windows leading into the patio. Flanking these windows are low bookcases. In the back wall is, right, a closet door; and, centre, a table holding a wine decanter and glasses. The left wall has a door upstage, and downstage a writing-desk with a straight chair in front of it. Near the desk is an arm-chair. Down right is a small sofa with a table holding a lamp at the upstage end of it. There are pictures on the walls. The room looks rather stuffy and unlived in.*

When the curtains part, the stage is in darkness save for the moonlight that comes through the french windows. Then the house door opens and a young girl in négligé enters stealthily. She is carrying a lighted candle. She stands at the door a moment listening for possible pursuit, then moves quickly across to the bookcase down right. She puts the candle on top of the bookcase and begins searching behind the books. She finally finds what she wants: a small bottle. While she is searching, the house door opens silently, and a woman, also in négligé, enters. She moves silently across the room to the table by the sofa, and as the girl turns with the bottle, the woman switches on the light. The girl gives a half-scream and draws back, frightened. The light reveals her to be quite young – no more than twenty – a timid, dove-like creature. The woman has a queenly air, and whether she is actually beautiful or not, people think she is. She is about thirty-two.

MARICA (*trying to hide the bottle behind her*). Raquel! What are you doing here?

RAQUEL. What have you hidden behind the books, Marica?

115

MARICA (*attempting a forced laugh*).   I? Nothing. Why do you think I have anything?

RAQUEL (*taking a step towards her*).   Give it to me.

MARICA (*backing away from her*).   No. No, I won't.

RAQUEL (*stretching out her hand*).   I demand that you give it to me.

MARICA.   You have no right to order me about. I'm a married woman. I ... I ... (*She begins to sob, and flings herself down on the sofa.*)

RAQUEL (*much gentler*).   You shouldn't be up. The doctor told you to stay in bed. (*She bends over Marica and gently takes the bottle out of the girl's hand.*) It was poison. I thought so.

MARICA (*frightened*).   You won't tell the priest, will you?

RAQUEL.   Suicide is a sin, Marica. A sin against God.

MARICA.   I know. I ... (*She catches* RAQUEL's *hand.*) Oh, Raquel, why do we have to have wars? Why do men have to go to war and be killed?

RAQUEL.   Men must fight for what they believe is right. It is an honourable thing to die for your country as a soldier!

MARICA.   How can you say that with Domingo out there fighting, too? And fighting what? Men who aren't even men. Peasants. Ranch slaves. Men who shouldn't be allowed to fight.

RAQUEL.   Peasants are men, Marica. Not animals.

MARICA.   Men. It's always men. But how about the women? What becomes of us?

RAQUEL.   We can pray.

MARICA (*bitterly*).   Yes, we can pray. And then comes the terrible news, and it's no use praying any more. All the reason for our praying is dead. Why would I go on living with Tomas dead?

RAQUEL.   Living is a duty.

MARICA.   How can you be so cold, so hard? You are a cold

and hard woman, Raquel. My brother worships you. He has never even looked at another woman since the first day he saw you. Does he know how cold and hard you are?

RAQUEL. Domingo is my – honoured husband.

MARICA. You've been married for ten years. And I've been married for three months. If Domingo is killed, it won't be the same for you. You've had ten years. (*She is crying wildly.*) I haven't anything – anything at all.

RAQUEL. You've had three months – three months of laughter. And now you have tears. How lucky you are. You have tears. Perhaps five months of tears. Not more. You're only twenty. And in five months Tomas will become just a lovely memory.

MARICA. I'll remember Tomas all my life.

RAQUEL. Of course. But he'll be distant and far away. But you're young – and the young need laughter. The young can't live on tears. And one day in Paris, or Rome, or even Mexico City, you'll meet another man. You'll marry again. There will be children in your house. How lucky you are.

MARICA. I'll never marry again.

RAQUEL. You're only twenty. You'll think differently when you're twenty-eight, or thirty.

MARICA. What will you do if Domingo is killed?

RAQUEL. I shall be very proud that he died in all his courage … in all the greatness of a hero.

MARICA. But you'd not weep, would you? Not you! I don't think there are any tears in you.

RAQUEL. No. I'd not weep. I'd sit here in this empty house and wait.

MARICA. Wait for what?

RAQUEL. For the jingle of his spurs as he walks across the tiled hall. For the sound of his laughter in the patio. For the echo of his voice as he shouts to the groom to put away his horse. For the feel of his hand …

MARICA (*screams*). Stop it!

RAQUEL. I'm sorry.

MARICA. You do love him, don't you?

RAQUEL. I don't think even he knows how much.

MARICA. I thought that after ten years people slid away from love. But you and Domingo — why, you're all he thinks about. When he's away from you he talks about you all the time. I heard him say once that when you were out of his sight he was like a man without eyes or ears or hands.

RAQUEL. I know. I, too, know that feeling.

MARICA. Then how could you let him go to war? Perhaps to be killed? How could you?

RAQUEL (*sharply*). Marica, you are of the family Macías. Your family is a family of great warriors. A Macías man was with Ferdinand when the Moors were driven out of Spain. A Macías man was with Cortes when the Aztecans surrendered. Your grandfather fought in the War of Independence. Your own father was executed not twenty miles from this house by the French. Shall his son be any less brave because he loves a woman?

MARICA. But Domingo loved you enough to forget that. If you had asked him, he wouldn't have gone to war. He would have stayed here with you.

RAQUEL. No, he would not have stayed. Your brother is a man of honour, not a whining, creeping, coward.

MARICA (*beginning to cry again*). I begged Tomas not to go. I begged him.

RAQUEL. Would you have loved him if he had stayed?

MARICA. I don't know. I don't know.

RAQUEL. There is your answer. You'd have despised him. Loved and despised him. Now come, Marica, it's time for you to go to bed.

MARICA. You won't tell the priest — about the poison, I mean?

RAQUEL. No. I won't tell him.

MARICA.   Thank you, Raquel. How good you are. How kind and good.

RAQUEL.   A moment ago I was hard and cruel. What a baby you are! Now, off to bed with you.

MARICA.   Aren't you coming upstairs too?

RAQUEL.   No ... I haven't been sleeping very well lately. I think I'll read for a little while.

MARICA.   Good night, Raquel. And thank you.

RAQUEL.   Good night, little one.

> (MARICA *goes out through the house door left, taking her candle with her.* RAQUEL *stares down at the bottle of poison in her hand, then puts it away in one of the small drawers of the desk. She next selects a book from the downstage case, and sits on the sofa to read it, but feeling chilly, she rises and goes to the closet, back right, and takes out an afghan. Coming back to the sofa, she makes herself comfortable, with the afghan across her knees. Suddenly she hears a noise in the patio. She listens, then, convinced it is nothing, returns to her reading. But she hears the noise again. She goes out to the patio door and peers out.*)

RAQUEL (*calling softly*).   Who's there? Who's out there? Oh! (*She gasps and backs into the room. Two men — or rather a man and a young boy — dressed in the white pyjama suits of the Mexican peasants, with their sombreros tipped low over their faces, come into the room.* RAQUEL *draws herself up regally. Her voice is cold and commanding.*) Who are you, and what do you want here?

ANDRES.   We are hunting for the wife of General Macías.

RAQUEL.   I am Raquel Rivera de Macías.

ANDRES.   Cleto, stand guard in the patio. If you hear any suspicious noise, warn me at once.

CLETO.   Yes, my captain. (*The boy returns to the patio.*)

*(The man, hooking his thumbs in his belt, strolls
around the room, looking it over. When he reaches
the table at the back he sees the wine. With a small
bow to* RAQUEL *he pours himself a glass of wine and
drains it. He wipes his mouth with the back of his
hand.)*

RAQUEL.   How very interesting.

ANDRES *(startled)*.   What?

RAQUEL.   To be able to drink wine with that hat on.

ANDRES.   The hat? Oh, forgive me, senora. *(He flicks the
brim with his fingers so that it drops off his head and dangles
down his back from the neck cord.)* In a military camp one
forgets one's polite manners. Would you care to join me in
another glass?

RAQUEL *(sitting on sofa)*.   Why not? It's my wine.

ANDRES.   And very excellent wine. *(He pours two glasses
and gives her one while he is talking.)* I would say Amontillado
of the vintage of 'eighty-seven.

RAQUEL.   Did you learn that in a military camp?

ANDRES.   I used to sell wines … among other things.

RAQUEL *(ostentatiously hiding a yawn)*.   I am devastated.

ANDRES *(pulls over the arm-chair and makes himself comfortable in it.)* You don't mind, do you?

RAQUEL.   Would it make any difference if I did?

ANDRES.   No. The Federals are searching the streets for us
and we have to stay somewhere. But women of your class
seem to expect that senseless sort of question.

RAQUEL.   Of course I suppose I could scream.

ANDRES.   Naturally.

RAQUEL.   My sister-in-law is upstairs asleep. And there are
several servants in the back of the house. Mostly men servants.
Very big men.

ANDRES.   Very interesting. *(He is drinking the wine in small
sips with much enjoyment.)*

RAQUEL. What would you do if I screamed?

ANDRES (*considering the request as though it were another glass of wine*). Nothing.

RAQUEL. I am afraid you are lying to me.

ANDRES. Women of your class seem to expect polite little lies.

RAQUEL. Stop calling me 'woman of your class'.

ANDRES. Forgive me.

RAQUEL. You are one of the fighting peasants, aren't you?

ANDRES. I am a captain of the Revolutionary Army.

RAQUEL. This house is completely loyal to the Federal Government.

ANDRES. I know. That is why I'm here.

RAQUEL. And now that you are here, just what do you expect me to do?

ANDRES. I expect you to offer sanctuary to myself and Cleto.

RAQUEL. Cleto? (*She looks towards the patio and adds sarcastically.*) Oh, your army.

CLETO (*appearing in the doorway*). I'm sorry, my captain. I just heard a noise. (RAQUEL *stands.* ANDRES *moves quickly to her and puts his hands on her arms from the back.* CLETO *has turned and is peering into the patio. Then the boy relaxes.*) We are still safe, my captain. It was only a rabbit. (*He goes back into the patio.* RAQUEL *pulls away from* ANDRES *and goes to the desk.*)

RAQUEL. What a magnificent army you have. So clever. I'm sure you must win many victories.

ANDRES. We do. And we will win the greatest victory, remember that.

RAQUEL. This farce has gone on long enough. Will you please take your army and climb over the patio wall with it?

ANDRES. I told you that we came here so that you could give us sanctuary.

RAQUEL. My dear captain — captain without a name ...

ANDRES.   Andres de la O, your servant. (*He makes a bow.*)

RAQUEL (*startled*).   Andres de la O!

ANDRES.   I am flattered. You have heard of me?

RAQUEL.   Naturally. Everyone in the city has heard of you. You have a reputation for politeness — especially to women.

ANDRES.   I see that the tales about me have lost nothing in the telling.

RAQUEL.   I can't say. I'm not interested in gossip about your type of soldier.

ANDRES.   Then let me give you something to heighten your interest. (*He suddenly takes her in his arms and kisses her. She stiffens for a moment, then remains perfectly still. He steps away from her.*)

RAQUEL (*rage forcing her to whisper*).   Get out of here — at once!

ANDRES (*staring at her in admiration*).   I can understand why Macías loves you. I couldn't before, but now I understand it.

RAQUEL.   Get out of my house.

ANDRES (*sits on the sofa and pulls a small leather pouch out of his shirt. He pours its contents into his hands.*)   So cruel, senora, and I with a present for you? Here is a holy medal. My mother gave me this medal. She died when I was ten. She was a street beggar. She died of starvation. But I wasn't there. I was in gaol. I had been sentenced to five years in prison for stealing five oranges. The judge thought it a great joke. One year for each orange. He laughed. He had a very loud laugh. (*Pauses.*) I killed him two months ago. I hanged him to the telephone pole in front of his house. And I laughed. (*Pause.*) I also have a very loud laugh. (RAQUEL *abruptly turns her back on him.*) I told that story to a girl the other night and she thought it very funny. But of course she was a peasant girl — a girl who could neither read nor write. She hadn't been born in a great house in Tabasco. She didn't have an English governess. She didn't go to school to the nuns in Paris. She didn't marry one of the richest young men in the Republic. But she thought my story very funny. Of course she could understand it. Her brother had been whipped to death because he had run away from the plantation that owned him. (*He pauses and looks at her. She does not move.*) Are you still angry with me? Even though I have brought you a present? (*He holds out his hand.*) A very nice present — from your husband.

RAQUEL (*turns and stares at him in amazement*). A present! From Domingo?

ANDRES. I don't know him that well. I call him the General Macías.

RAQUEL (*excitedly*). Is he well? How does he look? (*With horrified comprehension.*) He's a prisoner ... your prisoner!

ANDRES. Naturally. That's why I know so much about you. He talks about you constantly.

RAQUEL. You know nothing about him. You're lying to me.
        (CLETO *comes to the window.*)

ANDRES. I assure you, senora ...

CLETO (*interrupting*). My captain ...

ANDRES. What is it, Cleto? Another rabbit?

CLETO. No, my captain. There are soldiers at the end of the street. They are searching all the houses. They will be here soon.

ANDRES. Don't worry. We are quite safe here. Stay in the patio until I call you.

CLETO. Yes, my captain. (*He returns to the patio.*)

RAQUEL. You are not safe here. When those soldiers come I shall turn you over to them.

ANDRES. I think not.

RAQUEL. You can't escape from them. And they are not kind to you peasant prisoners. They have good reason not to be.

ANDRES. Look at this ring. (*He holds out his hand, with the ring on his palm.*)

RAQUEL. Why, it's a wedding ring.

ANDRES. Read the inscription inside of it. (*As she hesitates, he adds sharply.*) Read it!

RAQUEL (*slowly takes the ring. While she is reading her voice fades to a whisper.*) 'D.M. – R.R. – June 2, 1902.' Where did you get this?

ANDRES. General Macías gave it to me.

RAQUEL (*firmly and clearly*). Not this ring. He'd never give you this ring. (*With dawning horror.*) He's dead. You stole it from his dead finger. He's dead.

ANDRES. Not yet. But he will be dead if I don't return to camp safely by sunset tomorrow.

RAQUEL. I don't believe you. I don't believe you. You're lying to me.

ANDRES. This house is famous for its loyalty to the Federal Government. You will hide me until those soldiers get out of the district. When it is safe enough Cleto and I will leave. But if you betray me to them, your husband will be shot tomorrow evening at sunset. Do you understand? (*He shakes her arm.* RAQUEL *looks dazedly at him.* CLETO *comes to the window.*)

CLETO. The soldiers are coming closer, my captain. They are at the next house.

ANDRES (*to* RAQUEL). Where shall we hide? (RAQUEL *is still dazed. He gives her another little shake.*) Think, woman! If you love your husband at all – think!

RAQUEL. I don't know. Marica upstairs – the servants in the rest of the house – I don't know.

ANDRES. The General has bragged to us about you. He says that you are braver than most men. He says that you are very clever. This is a time to be both brave and clever.

CLETO (*pointing to the closet*). What door is that?

RAQUEL. It's a closet ... a storage closet.

ANDRES. We'll hide in there.

RAQUEL. It's very small. It's not big enough for both of you.

ANDRES. Cleto, hide yourself in there.

CLETO. But, my captain ...

ANDRES. That's an order! Hide yourself.

CLETO. Yes, sir. (*He steps inside the closet.*)

ANDRES. And now, senora, where are you going to hide me?

RAQUEL. How did you persuade my husband to give you this ring?

ANDRES. That's a very long story, senora, for which we have no time just now. (*He puts the ring and medal back in the pouch and thrusts it inside his shirt.*) Later I will be glad to give you all the details. But at present it is only necessary for you to remember that his life depends upon mine.

RAQUEL. Yes — yes, of course. (*She loses her dazed expression and seems to grow more queenly as she takes command of the situation.*) Give me your hat. (ANDRES *shrugs and passes it over to her. She takes it to the closet and hands it to* CLETO.) There is a smoking-jacket hanging up in there. Hand it to me. (CLETO *hands her a man's velvet smoking-jacket. She brings it to* ANDRES.) Put this on.

ANDRES (*puts it on and looks down at himself*). Such a pity my shoes are not comfortable slippers.

RAQUEL. Sit in that chair. (*She points to the arm-chair.*)

ANDRES. My dear lady ...

RAQUEL. If I must save your life, allow me to do it my own way. Sit down. (ANDRES *sits. She picks up the afghan from the couch and throws it over his feet and legs, carefuly tucking it in so that his body is covered to the waist.*) If anyone speaks to you, don't answer. Don't turn your head. As far as you are concerned, there is no one in this room — not even me. Just look straight ahead of you and ...

ANDRES (*as she pauses*). And what?

RAQUEL. I started to say 'and pray', but since you're a member of the Revolutionary Army I don't suppose you believe in God and prayer.

ANDRES.   My mother left me a holy medal.

RAQUEL.   Oh, yes, I remember. A very amusing story. (*There is the sound of men's voices in the patio.*) The Federal soldiers are here. If you can pray, ask God to keep Marica upstairs. She is very young and very stupid. She'll betray you before I can shut her mouth.

ANDRES.   I'll ...

RAQUEL.   Silence! Stare straight ahead of you and pray. (*She goes to the french windows and speaks loudly to the soldiers.*) Really! What is the meaning of this uproar?

FLORES (*off*).   Do not alarm yourself, senora. (*He comes into the room, wearing the uniform of a Federal officer.*) I am Captain Basilio Flores, at your service, senora.

RAQUEL.   What do you mean, invading my house and making so much noise at this hour of the night?

FLORES.   We are hunting for two spies. One of them is the notorious Andres de la O. You may have heard of him, senora.

RAQUEL (*looking at* ANDRES).   Considering what he did to my cousin — yes, I've heard of him.

FLORES.   Your cousin, senora?

RAQUEL (*comes to* ANDRES *and puts her hand on his shoulder. He stares woodenly in front of him*).   Felipe was his prisoner before the poor boy managed to escape.

FLORES.   Is it possible? (*He crosses to* ANDRES.) Captain Basilio Flores at your service. (*He salutes.*)

RAQUEL.   Felipe doesn't hear you. He doesn't even know you are in the room.

FLORES.   Eh, it is a sad thing.

RAQUEL.   Must your men make so much noise?

FLORES.   The hunt must be thorough, senora. And now if some of my men can go through here to the rest of the house ...

RAQUEL.   Why?

FLORES.   But I told you, senora. We are hunting for two spies ...

RAQUEL (*speaking quickly from controlled nervousness*). And do you think I have them hidden some place, and I the wife of General Macías?

FLORES.   General Macías! But I didn't know ...

RAQUEL.   Now that you do know, I suggest you remove your men and their noise at once.

FLORES.   But, senora, I regret — I still have to search this house.

RAQUEL.   I can assure you, Captain, that I have been sitting here all evening, and no peasant spy has passed me and gone into the rest of the house.

FLORES.   Several rooms open off the patio, senora. They needn't have come through here.

RAQUEL.   So ... you do think I conceal spies in this house. Then search it by all means. Look under the sofa ... under the table. In the drawers of the desk. And don't miss that closet, captain. Inside that closet is hidden a very fierce and wicked spy.

FLORES.   Please, senora ...

RAQUEL (*goes to the closet door*).   Or do you prefer me to open it for you?

FLORES.   I am only doing my duty, senora. You are making it very difficult.

RAQUEL (*relaxing against the door*).   I'm sorry. My sister-in-law is upstairs. She has just received word that her husband has been killed. They were married three months ago. I didn't want ...

MARICA (*calling off*).   Raquel, what is all that noise down-stairs?

RAQUEL (*goes to the house door and calls*).   It is nothing. Go back to bed.

MARICA.   But I can hear men's voices in the patio.

RAQUEL.   It is only some Federal soldiers hunting for two peasant spies. (*She turns and speaks to* FLORES.) If she comes down here, she must not see my cousin. Felipe escaped, but her husband was killed. The doctor thinks the sight of my poor cousin might affect her mind. You understand?

FLORES.   Certainly, senora. What a sad thing.

MARICA (*still off*).   Raquel, I'm afraid! (*She tries to push past* RAQUEL *into the room.* RAQUEL *and* FLORES *stand between her and* ANDRES.) Spies! In this house. Oh, Raquel!

RAQUEL.   The doctor will be very angry if you don't return to bed at once.

MARICA.   But those terrible men will kill us. What is the matter with you two? Why are you standing there like that? (*She tries to see past them, but they both move so that she can't see* ANDRES.)

FLORES.   It is better that you go back to your room, senora.

MARICA.   But why? Upstairs I am alone. Those terrible men will kill me. I know they will.

FLORES.   Don't be afraid, senora. There are no spies in this house.

MARICA.   Are you sure?

RAQUEL.   Captain Flores means that no spy would dare to take refuge in the house of General Macías. Isn't that right, Captain?

FLORES (*laughing*).   Of course. All the world knows of the brave General Macías.

RAQUEL.   Now go back to bed, Marica. Please, for my sake.

MARICA.   You are both acting very strangely. I think you have something hidden in this room you don't want me to see.

RAQUEL (*sharply*).   You are quite right. Captain Flores has captured one of the spies. He is sitting in the chair behind me. He is dead. Now will you please go upstairs!

MARICA (*gives a stifled sob*).   Oh! That such a terrible thing could happen in this house! (*She runs out of the room, still sobbing.*)

FLORES.   Was it wise to tell her such a story, senora?

RAQUEL (*tense with repressed relief*).   Better that than the truth. Good night, Captain, and thank you.

FLORES.   Good night, senora. And don't worry. Those spies won't bother you. If they were anywhere in this district, my men would have found them.

RAQUEL.   I'm sure of it.

> (*The Captain salutes her, looks towards* ANDRES *and salutes him, then goes into the patio. He can be heard calling his men. Neither* ANDRES *nor* RAQUEL *moves until the voices outside die away. Then* RAQUEL *staggers and nearly falls, but* ANDRES *catches her in time.*)

ANDRES (*calling softly*).   They've gone, Cleto. (ANDRES *carries* RAQUEL *to the sofa as* CLETO *comes out of the closet.*) Bring a glass of wine. Quickly.

CLETO (*as he gets the wine*).   What happened?

ANDRES.   It's nothing. Just a faint. (*He holds the wine to her lips.*)

CLETO.   She's a great lady, that one. When she wanted to open the closet door my knees were trembling, I can tell you.

ANDRES.   My own bones were playing a pretty tune.

CLETO.   Why do you think she married Macías?

ANDRES.   Love is a peculiar thing, Cleto.

CLETO.   I don't understand it.

RAQUEL (*moans and sits up*).   Are they — are they gone?

ANDRES.   Yes, they're gone. (*He kisses her hand.*) I've never known a braver lady.

RAQUEL (*pulling her hand away.*)   Will you go now, please?

ANDRES.   We'll have to wait until the district is free of them -- but if you'd like to write a letter to your husband while we're waiting —

RAQUEL (*surprised at his kindness*).   You'd take it to him? You'd really give it to him?

ANDRES.   Of course.

RAQUEL.   Thank you. (*She goes to the writing-desk and sits down.*)

ANDRES (*to* CLETO, *who has been staring steadily at* RAQUEL *all the while*).   You stay here with the senora. I'm going to find out how much of the district has been cleared.

CLETO (*still staring at* RAQUEL).   Yes, my captain.

> (ANDRES *leaves by the french windows.* CLETO *keeps on staring at* RAQUEL *as she starts to write. After a moment she turns to him.*)

RAQUEL (*irritated*).   Why do you keep staring at me?

CLETO.   Why did you marry a man like that one, senora?

RAQUEL.   You're very impertinent.

CLETO (*shyly*).   I'm sorry, senora.

RAQUEL (*after a brief pause*).   What do you mean: 'A man like that one'?

CLETO.   Well, you're very brave, senora.

RAQUEL (*lightly*).   And don't you think the general is very brave?

CLETO.   No, senora. Not very.

RAQUEL (*staring at him with bewilderment*).   What are you trying to tell me?

CLETO.   Nothing, senora. It is none of my affair.

RAQUEL.   Come here. (*He comes slowly up to her.*) Tell me what is in your mind.

CLETO.   I don't know, senora. I don't understand it. The captain says love is a peculiar thing, but I don't understand it.

RAQUEL.   Cleto, did the general willingly give that ring to your captain?

CLETO.   Yes, senora.

RAQUEL.   Why?

CLETO.   The general wanted to save his own life. He said he loved you and he wanted to save his life.

RAQUEL.   How would giving that ring to your captain save the general's life?

CLETO. The general's supposed to be shot tomorrow afternoon. But he's talked about you a lot, and when my captain knew we had to come into the city, he thought perhaps we might take refuge here if the Federals got on our trail. So he went to the general and said that if he fixed it so we'd be safe here, my captain would save him from the firing squad.

RAQUEL. Was your trip here to the city very important – to your cause, I mean?

CLETO. Indeed yes, senora. The captain got a lot of fine information. It means we'll win the next big battle. My captain is a very clever man, senora.

RAQUEL. Did the general know about this information when he gave the ring to your captain?

CLETO. I don't see how he could help knowing it, senora. He heard us talking about it enough.

RAQUEL. Who knows about that bargain to save the general's life besides you and your captain?

CLETO. No one, senora. The captain isn't one to talk, and I didn't have time to.

RAQUEL (*while the boy has been talking, the life seems to have drained completely out of her*). How old are you, Cleto?

CLETO. I don't know, senora. I think I'm twenty, but I don't know.

RAQUEL (*speaking more to herself than to him*). Tomas was twenty.

CLETO. Who is Tomas?

RAQUEL. He was married to my sister-in-law. Cleto, you think my husband is a coward, don't you?

CLETO (*with embarrassment*). Yes, senora.

RAQUEL. You don't think any woman is worth it, do you? Worth the price of a great battle, I mean?

CLETO. No, senora. But as the captain says, love is a very peculiar thing.

RAQUEL. If your captain loved a woman as much as the general loves me, would he have given an enemy his ring?

CLETO. Ah, but the captain is a great man, senora.

RAQUEL. And so is my husband a great man. He is of the family Macías. All of that family have been great men. All of them – brave and honourable men. They have always held their honour to be greater than their lives. That is a tradition of their family.

CLETO. Perhaps none of them loved a woman like you, senora.

RAQUEL. How strange you are. I saved you from the Federals because I want to save my husband's life. You call me brave and yet you call him a coward. There is no difference in what we have done.

CLETO. But you are a woman, senora.

RAQUEL. Has a woman less honour than a man, then?

CLETO. No, senora. Please, I don't know how to say it. The general is a soldier. He has a duty to his own cause. You are a woman. You have a duty to your husband. It is right that you should try to save him. It is not right that he should try to save himself.

RAQUEL (*dully*). Yes, of course. It is right that I should save him. (*Becoming practical again.*) Your captain has been gone some time, Cleto. You'd better find out if he is still safe.

CLETO. Yes, senora. (*As he reaches the french windows she stops him.*)

RAQUEL. Wait, Cleto. Have you a mother – or a wife, perhaps?

CLETO. Oh, no, senora. I haven't anyone but the captain.

RAQUEL. But the captain is a soldier. What would you do if he should be killed?

CLETO. It is very simple, senora. I should be killed too.

RAQUEL. You speak about death so calmly. Aren't you afraid of it, Cleto?

CLETO. No, senora. It's like the captain says ... dying for what you believe in, that's the finest death of all.

RAQUEL. And you believe in the Revolutionary cause?

CLETO. Yes, senora. I am a poor peasant, that's true. But still I have a right to live like a man, with my own ground, and my own family, and my own future. (*He stops speaking abruptly.*) I'm sorry, senora. You are a fine lady. You don't understand these things. I must go and find my captain. (*He goes out.*)

RAQUEL (*rests her face against her hand*). He's so young. But Tomas was no older. And he's not afraid. He said so. Oh, Domingo — Domingo! (*She straightens abruptly, takes the bottle of poison from the desk drawer and stares at it. Then she crosses to the decanter and laces the wine with the poison. She hurries back to the desk and is busy writing when* ANDRES *and* CLETO *return.*)

ANDRES. You'll have to hurry that letter. The district is clear now.

RAQUEL. I'll be through in just a moment. You might as well finish the wine while you're waiting.

ANDRES. Thank you. A most excellent idea. (*He pours himself a glass of wine. As he lifts it to his lips, she speaks.*)

RAQUEL. Why don't you give some to — Cleto?

ANDRES. This is too fine a wine to waste on that boy.

RAQUEL. He'll probably never have another chance to taste such wine.

ANDRES. Very well. Pour yourself a glass, Cleto.

CLETO. Thank you. (*He pours it.*) Your health, my captain.

RAQUEL (*quickly*). Drink it outside, Cleto. I want to speak to your captain. (*The boy looks at* ANDRES, *who jerks his head towards the patio.* CLETO *nods and goes out.*) I want you to give my husband a message for me. I can't write it. You'll have to remember it. But first, give me a glass of wine too.

ANDRES (*pouring the wine*). It might be easier for him if you wrote it.

RAQUEL. I think not. (*She takes the glass.*) I want you to tell him that I never knew how much I loved him until tonight.

ANDRES. Is that all?

RAQUEL. Yes. Tell me, Captain, do you think it possible to love a person too much?

ANDRES. Yes, senora, I do.

RAQUEL. So do I. Let us drink a toast, Captain, to Honour. To bright and shining Honour.

ANDRES (*raises his glass*). To Honour. (*He drains his glass. She lifts hers almost to her lips and then puts it down. From the patio comes a faint cry.*)

CLETO (*calling faintly in a cry that fades into silence*). Captain. Captain.

> (ANDRES *sways, his hand trying to brush across his face as though trying to brush sense into his head. When he hears* CLETO *he tries to stagger towards the window, but stumbles and can't quite make it. Hanging on to the table by the sofa he looks accusingly at her. She shrinks back against the chair.*)

ANDRES (*his voice weak from the poison*). Why?

RAQUEL. Because I love him. Can you understand that?

ANDRES. We'll win. The Revolution will win. You can't stop that.

RAQUEL. Yes, you'll win. I know that now.

ANDRES. That girl – she thought my story was funny – about the hanging. But you didn't ...

RAQUEL. I'm glad you hanged him. I'm glad.

> (ANDRES *looks at her and tries to smile. He manages to pull the pouch from his shirt and extend it to her. But it drops from his hand.*)

RAQUEL (*runs to french window and calls*). Cleto. Cleto! (*She buries her face in her hands for a moment, then comes back to* ANDRES. *She kneels beside him and picks up the leather pouch. She opens it and, taking the ring, puts it on her finger. Then she sees the medal. She rises and, pulling out the chain from her own throat, she slides the medal on to the chain. Then she walks to the sofa and sinks down on it.*

MARICA (*calling off*).   Raquel! Raquel! (RAQUEL *snaps off the lamp, leaving the room in darkness.* MARICA *opens the house door. She is carrying a candle which she shades with her hand. The light is too dim to reveal the dead* ANDRES.) What are you doing down here in the dark? Why don't you come to bed?

RAQUEL (*making an effort to speak*).   I'll come in just a moment.

MARICA.   But what are you doing, Raquel?

RAQUEL.   Nothing. Just listening – listening to an empty house.

QUICK CURTAIN

THREE TO GET MARRIED

A drama for television

by

KAY HILL

CHARACTERS

Rev. Horatio Dogberry
Angelina
Seraphina
Dulcinea
Aunt Lizzie
Tom Oates
Chester Greengate
Lieutenant Honeywell
Scarecrow Man
Will Kane

SETS: Wood, or garden, near rectory. Exterior church.
Living-room of rectory. Kitchen of rectory

Scene I

MUSIC: *Period piece, springlike and sprightly.*

FADE IN ON GARDEN, OR WOOD, NEAR RECTORY.

(REV. HORATIO DOGBERRY *meanders through the wood happily, beaming around with approval at the trees and birds.*)

HORATIO. Ah, the spring sun – the fragrance of apple blossom – and (*ruefully dragging one foot out of the mud and looking at it*) the good soil! There's really nothing like spring in Nova Scotia – eh, my little feathered brother? (*Calling over shoulder.*) Come, Angelina – Seraphina – Dulcinea – (*Picks flower and examines it with interest.*)

> (ANGELINA *and* SERAPHINA *pick their way distastefully through mud, holding up skirts.* SERAPHINA *makes for the log and sits thankfully.* ANGELINA *stands on one foot, scraping mud off shoe of the other with stick.*

SERAPHINA (*disgustedly*). Spring!

ANGELINA. Mud!

HORATIO (*cheerfully*). Now for our next lesson.

ANGELINA. Oh, Papa, haven't we had enough biology for today?

HORATIO. My dears, I want all my daughters to – (*Pauses and looks around.*) But where is Dulcinea?

SERAPHINA. Picking mayflowers probably –

ANGELINA. Or quoting Shelley to a bullfrog!

HORATIO (*looking off anxiously*). Biology is her favourite subject.

139

ANGELINA *and* SERAPHINA (*quick glance at each other*).   Oh — ours too, Papa.

HORATIO.   Very well. As you know, biology is the study of life — including man.

ANGELINA (*yearningly*).   *Especially* man!

HORATIO (*absorbed in his lecture, not really hearing the girls*). Specimens of life are all around us —

SERAPHINA (*acidly*).   *Excepting* man!

HORATIO.   The great difference being that plants are stationary —

ANGELINA (*gloomily*).   Like us.

HORATIO.   And remain in their natural habitat.

SERAPHINA.   A poor country rectory!

HORATIO.   Animals, on the other hand, move about.

ANGELINA (*enviously*).   As men do!

SERAPHINA.   Only not around *us*, unfortunately!

HORATIO.   Observe the stamens and pistils — (SERAPHINA *gives* ANGELINA *a nudge, but* ANGELINA *shakes her head and pantomimes 'you do it'*.) — for male and female cells must come together.

SERAPHINA (*rising and cutting in boldly*).   Like getting married, Papa.

ANGELINA (*rising too*).   Only what if they never do — come together, I mean?

HORATIO.   Well, sometimes there are barriers — rivers, oceans —

SERAPHINA.   Roads blocked with mud —

ANGELINA.   No near neighbours —

SERAPHINA.   No pretty clothes!

HORATIO.   In which case — (*Pause.*) (*Puzzled.*) Clothes?

ANGELINA (*hastily sitting down*).   You spoke of barriers, Papa! (SERAPHINA *glares at her.*)

HORATIO.   Yes — in which case — (*Pause.*) (*Puzzled.*) Clothes?

ANGELINA (*jumping up eagerly*). There must be many churches in Halifax and Saint John in need of ministers!

HORATIO (*bewildered*). Churches? Ministers? Why, my dear child, I am content here.

SERAPHINA. But —

HORATIO (*catching sight of* DULCINEA). Ah — there you are, Dulcinea. (*Pulls out watch.*) Bless my soul! It's past dinner-time. Aunt Lizzie will think we are lost.

> (HORATIO *hurries off towards rectory as* DULCINEA *comes dreamily from opposite direction.*)

HORATIO. Come along —

SERAPHINA (*to* ANGELINA). Coward!

ANGELINA (*tossing her head*). You've got a tongue too!

HORATIO (*off*). Girls!

ANGELINA (*calling*). Coming, Papa. (*To* DULCINEA *walking carelessly through mud.*) Mind your shoes, Dulcie!

SERAPHINA (*picking her way daintily*). What kept you?

DULCINEA (*dreamily*). A handsome knight on horseback.

ANGELINA (*whirling*). What!

SERAPHINA (*splashing back through mud*). Where?

ANGELINA (*urgently at* DULCINEA'S *other side*). When?

DULCINEA (*surprised*). Just now — on the Windsor Road.

SERAPHINA (*excitedly*). Do you suppose he's stopping near?

ANGELINA. Not likely. There's no inn closer than Annapolis.

SERAPHINA. What was he like?

DULCINEA. Young — and handsome.

ANGELINA. How was he dressed?

DULCINEA. In a green suit — and yellow hose —

SERAPHINA (*indignantly*). What!

ANGELINA (*angrily*). Oh, for heaven's sake — you mean that shabby pedlar!

DULCINEA. I suppose — yes, he had a pack on his back.

ANGELINA (*switching away angrily*). Knight indeed!

SERAPHINA. Pedlars and hired men! They're all the men we

ever see! (*Turning to* ANGELINA *as she stalks off.*) Angelina, we've got to *do* something.

ANGELINA (*going off with her*). Yes, something *must* be done.

DULCINEA (*softly*). Still — he *was* handsome. (*With a little skip as she runs off after others.*) Oh — isn't spring wonderful!

SUPER TITLE OVER AND FADE IN EXTERIOR CHURCH, WITH APPLE-TREE IN BLOOM. *Morning. Move in to show vegetables and live-stock on porch steps.*

SOUND: *Concluding verse of hymn sung by small number of voices, enthusiastically, but off key.*

PAN TO: *Tree trunk to show mile signs and* TOM OATES *entering from side. He marches to tree with parchment, which he unrolls with side glance at church. The hymn ends as he begins to tack up notice.*

CLOSE-UP OF PROCLAMATION (*or* TOM OATES *could stand back and read it aloud, admiringly*): 'On this 28th day of May, eighteen hundred and thirty-five, concerning the opening of a stage route to Annapolis ...'

SOUND: *Distant mutter of benediction, then murmur of voices as people issue from church.*

CUT TO: *Porch, where* HORATIO *is shaking hands with the last few members of congregation, beaming paternally at them.* THE GIRLS *and* AUNT LIZZIE *stand to one side surveying the array of vegetables, etc.*

HORATIO. Thank you, thank you — most kind. (*To* WOMEN.) Dear good-hearted souls. (*Beams after people fondly.*)

AUNT LIZZIE (*poking at cabbage with tip of umbrella*). So this is how country folk pay their ministers. Cash would be more practical. Soft! Cellar-rot! (*She picks it up and carries it off disdainfully.*) Come, girls —

ANGELINA. In a moment, Aunt Lizzie. Papa, is this all?

HORATIO (*surprised*).   All? Why, child, this will stock our pantry for weeks.

SERAPHINA.   But no cash?

HORATIO (*regretfully*).   Well, no. I fear money is scarce in our people's homes these days.

DULCINEA.   In ours, too.

ANGELINA (*crossly*).   You haven't been paid a penny in months.

HORATIO.   True. (*Cheerfully.*) Ah, well, the Lord will provide. Why, good gracious, there's Tom Oates from Kentville. What brings him this way? (*Hurrying off.*) Tom — I say, Tom!

DULCINEA.   Poor Papa. (*Picks up armful of provisions.*)

SERAPHINA (*picking up the lightest things, fastidiously*).   Poor us, you mean!

ANGELINA (*following the other two with armful of plucked chickens*).   The Lord may provide us with food, but unless He soon provides us with husbands, Papa will have three old maids on his hands — four, counting Aunt Lizzie!

CUT TO: *interior rectory (living-room). Same time.*

> (AUNT LIZZIE, *entering, sets down cabbage, goes to sofa with glint in her eye and reverses the two cushions on it. The girls prefer the fancy side; she likes the plain side. As she turns to go out to kitchen,* ANGELINA *and* SERAPHINA *enter and see the changed cushions.*)

AUNT LIZZIE.   Come along — time to get dinner.

> (ANGELINA *and* SERAPHINA *march to sofa and turn cushions back the way they like them.* DULCINEA *comes in and deposits her armload of provisions.*)

ANGELINA.   Papa doesn't realize!

SERAPHINA.   Then why don't we tell him!

ANGELINA (*primly*). It's not the sort of thing you discuss with a man! (*Sigh.*) If only dear Mama were alive!

DULCINEA. Anyway, what could Papa *do*?

ANGELINA. Exactly. It all comes down to money, and he hasn't got any money.

SERAPHINA (*hitting cushion*). Well, we all know who has some.

DULCINEA. Aunt Lizzie.

ANGELINA. Catch her lending any, even if Papa would ask.

SERAPHINA (*eyes gleaming*). *We* could ask!

ANGELINA (*gloomily*). Ask away, if you think it will do any earthly good. (*But she looks suddenly thoughtful, the girls stare at each other, suddenly hopeful.*)

SERAPHINA (*quickly*). You're the oldest, Angelina!

ANGELINA. Oh, but you're the charmer of the family!

SERAPHINA. Not with Aunt Lizzie! (*Turning on* DULCINEA.) Dulcinea's her favourite.

DULCINEA (*hastily, as they surround her*). *I* haven't noticed it. And I'm in no haste to marry anyway!

ANGELINA (*enviously*). *You're* young!

DULCINEA. I'm not sure I want to marry at all.

SERAPHINA *and* ANGELINA (*both shocked*). Dulcie!

ANGELINA. Ridiculous!

DULCINEA. Why is it ridiculous? Why must I always be told what to do by a man — first by Papa, and then by a husband? *Why* must I marry?

ANGELINA. Because it is the duty of a woman! A man must have a wife to run his household and raise his children.

SERAPHINA. A single woman has no fun, Dulcie — (*Thoughtfully.*) Unless she's a *naughty* single woman — (*Practically.*) — and *then* she has no *security*!

ANGELINA. It's also a matter of prestige. A woman alone has no *place* in life!

SERAPHINA. Look at Aunt Lizzie!

(*They all shudder.*)

SERAPHINA. For a well-brought-up woman, there's nothing else *but* marriage.

DULCINEA (*picking up half-plucked chicken and absently clutching it to her breast as she says soulfully and tenderly*). Just the same, if I do marry, it won't be for security or prestige — (*Softly, clasping the chicken.*) It will be for love!

SERAPHINA. Well, of *course*, he must be handsome and well-dressed.

DULCINEA. Wouldn't it be terrible to marry the wrong man?

ANGELINA (*grimly*). Better than no man at all!

SERAPHINA. A clever girl can get any man she wants — (*Meaningly.*) If she gets a chance to meet him, that is.

ANGELINA (*coaxingly*). That's why you must help us, Dulcie, dear. Won't you please try Aunt Lizzie, if only for *our* sakes?

DULCINEA (uneasily). I — oh, what could I *say*?

SERAPHINA (*eagerly*). That Papa is too poor to take us into society, and even if gentlemen visited us, we couldn't be seen in such poor gowns!

ANGELINA (*anxiously*). Fifty pounds, thirty even — would at least provide us with suitable clothes.

DULCINEA (*dubiously*). Well, I suppose I could try.

SERAPHINA (*hugging her*). Dearest girl!

ANGELINA (*as they move off with arms affectionately around* DULCINEA). After all, match-making is woman's business.

SERAPHINA. Aunt Lizzie ought to be glad to help —

CUT TO: *exterior church. Same time.*

HORATIO (*staring at sign*). And you say the stage will actually be in operation next month!

OATES (*proudly*). Yep! With me drivin'.

HORATIO.   But I don't quite understand about the inns. You say there aren't enough of them to take care of travellers?

OATES.   The way the roads is, we oughta have a stop every mile — just in case.

HORATIO.   There are many houses along the route.

OATES.   Well-off folks don't fancy turning their places into taverns, Minister. That's why gov'ment's offering this here twenty-five pounds — as encouragement-like.

HORATIO (*nodding*).   A sort of subsidy, I see. (*Reading.*) '... twenty-five pounds to any private householder on the Windsor road who will open his home to man and beast as an inn.'

OATES (*jokingly*).   So there's your chance.

HORATIO (*astonished*).   Eh? Me?

OATES (*hastily*).   Just funnin', sir. Parson couldn't hardly go in for innkeepin'.

HORATIO (*laughing*).   Dear me, no. Well — (*Seeing* OATES *gather his tools.*) Come and have a bite with us, Tom.

OATES (*shaking his head regretfully*).   I've et. Too bad. Them girls of yours is mighty fine cooks. Purty too. Queer they ain't been picked off.

HORATIO.   Picked off?

OATES.   Married.

HORATIO.   Oh, my dear fellow — those children? They're not thinking of marriage!

OATES.   Wouldn't bet on it, Minister. (*Touching cap as he moves off*).   Marryin' comes nat'ral to wimmin.

HORATIO (*waving absently*).   Good-bye then. (*Frowning.*) Marriage. Dear me — (*Pause.*) (*Brow clearing.*) But of course they're much too young.

CUT TO: *interior rectory (living-room). Same time.*

(AUNT LIZZIE *is being pursued around the room by*

a determined DULCINEA, *changing the cushions, etc.*)

AUNT LIZZIE.   You're much too young to think of marriage, Dulcinea!

DULCINEA.   But Angelina and Seraphina aren't — and they're getting desperate.

AUNT LIZZIE (*coldly*).   Desperate, fiddlesticks. *I've* got along well enough without a husband. Independence is a lot more satisfying!

DULCINEA (*casting about for ideas*).   But — what about duty? Isn't it a woman's duty to marry and have children?

AUNT LIZZIE (*outraged*).   Dulcinea — don't be vulgar.

DULCINEA (*desperately*).   And then there's prestige! Not having to depend on relations!

AUNT LIZZIE (*angrily*).   A woman with money *isn't* a dependant. (*Tightly.*) It's no use, I don't believe in lending money.

DULCINEA (*boldly*).   Then will you *give* it?

AUNT LIZZIE.   Give! Give! Great heavens, girl, you speak as if money were straw!

DULCINEA.   Only a little. (*Hopefully.*) Fifty pounds?

AUNT LIZZIE (*shrilly*).   Fifty! You might as well ask for a thousand.

DULCINEA.   But you're always saying you'll leave us the money —

AUNT LIZZIE (*stalking off upstairs*).   When I'm through with it — not before!

(DULCINEA *glares after her, stamps her foot.*)

CUT TO: *kitchen. Same time.*

SERAPHINA (*with her ear pressed to the wall*).   Bother! I can't hear a thing!

ANGELINA (*turning eagerly as* DULCINEA *comes flouncing in*). Well?

DULCINEA (*mimicking savagely*).   'When I'm through with it – not before!'

SERAPHINA (*despairingly*).   You mean – ?

ANGELINA.   She said 'No'.

DULCINEA.   I'm sorry, I did my best.

SERAPHINA.   I shall tell Papa to make her leave!

DULCINEA.   You know he wouldn't do that, Seraphina – not Mother's sister!

> (*They come into living-room. Find* HORATIO *in room as they enter.*)

SERAPHINA.   But if he knew how mean she is!

ANGELINA (*shaking her head*).   No, Dulcie's right. Papa seems mild, but nothing can move him from his principles.

SERAPHINA (*bitterly*).   Well, it's obvious Aunt Lizzie is here to stay. She's run out of relations who'll put up with her – (*Gasp.*) Why, no *wonder* she doesn't want us to get married!

ANGELINA (*indignantly*).   Of course! She knows once this home is broken up, she'd have to leave!

DULCINEA.   And she has it nice and soft here! Of all the sly, sneaky, heartless –

HORATIO.   Dulcinea!

> (*They jump and turn to see him rise, and flutter nervously as he looks at them in gentle reproof.*)

ANGELINA.   Papa – we didn't know –

SERAPHINA.   – you were there.

HORATIO.   May I ask what this is all about?

ANGELINA (*evasively*).   It's nothing, Papa.

HORATIO.   Now, now, my dear children –

SERAPHINA (*desperately*).   Well, look at us!

> (*They stand in a row before him, defiant, a little embarrassed.*)

HORATIO (*wonderingly*).   It just seems the other day – (*Pausing to take a very close look at* ANGELINA, *who covers the open neck of her dress with embarrassed modesty.*) Why, bless my soul! I believe you're right. Dear me, why didn't you mention it before?

ANGELINA (*weakly*). We thought —

DULCINEA. — you'd notice.

HORATIO. Yes, indeed, quite old enough to have homes of your own. (*Definitely.*) Marriage is woman's proper sphere. As Saint Paul said, 'It is better to marry than to burn.' And as it is most clearly shown in Isaiah, verse — (*Puzzled.*) verse — (*Smile.*) However, we'll take that as read. Now, what are we to do about it, eh? Invite some suitable young men?

(*Girls sit on sofa in row.*)

SERAPHINA (*despairingly*). What men?

ANGELINA. And we can't be seen like *this*!

HORATIO. Eh?

DULCINEA. You'd have to buy us new clothes and, Papa, clothes are expensive.

HORATIO (*struggling to grasp this elementary point*). Clothes? (*Worried.*) Are you sure clothes are *absolutely* necessary? (*At their solemn nods.*) Yes, yes, I see. Then we must purchase clothes. (*All lean forward eagerly.*) However, as I am presently situated — (*Girls sink back.*) I really don't quite see how — unless — (*Girls lean forward again.*) We must have faith! Faith moves mountains. (*Seeing them sigh and sit back discouraged.*) Of course, it may take a little time.

SERAPHINA. That's what we're running out of, Papa. Look at Angelina — lines around the mouth already.

ANGELINA (*turning her back angrily*). Thank you!

SERAPHINA. But it's really serious, Papa. Without you — what will become of us?

ANGELINA. Really, Seraphina!

HORATIO (*sitting down, really distressed*). No, no, Seraphina is right. I just hadn't thought of it before. Naturally I shan't live for ever, and I haven't a penny put by for my family. Oh, dear, oh dear!

DULCINEA (*running to Papa and hugging him*). Oh, we're selfish and unkind! Poor Papa, there's nothing he can do – he's poor because he never thinks of himself.

ANGELINA (*sighing*).   We're sorry, Papa.

SERAPHINA (*turning away*).   And that's that.

ANGELINA (*resignedly*).   After all, pound notes don't grow on trees.

(HORATIO *starts to nod, then looks startled*.)

HORATIO.   Trees!

DULCINEA (*soothingly*).   You mustn't worry –

HORATIO (*jumping to his feet excitedly*).   Trees! Of course! (*As they stare in amazement*.) Twenty-five pounds. Good gracious, the very thing. Ah, the Lord moves in a marvellous way His wonders to perform!

ANGELINA (*anxiously*).   What trees are you talking about?

HORATIO.   Why the one outside – the one with the proclamation. (*Girls look at each other fearfully, wondering if he's out of his mind*.)

SERAPHINA (*taking him by one arm and leading him to sofa*). Perhaps you'd better sit down, Papa.

ANGELINA (*taking the other arm*).   And we'll get you a nice cup of tea!

(*But no sooner is* HORATIO *almost down on the sofa than he leaps up again so suddenly that* ANGELINA *and* SERAPHINA *collapse on the sofa instead*.)

HORATIO.   I can't sit down! I've a great deal to do! My dears, I am about to become – an innkeeper! (*They stare at him as* AUNT LIZZIE *enters from kitchen*.)

AUNT LIZZIE.   Horatio, there's a pedlar at the door – on a Sunday too – (*Pause*.) (*Sharply*.) Innkeeper!

HORATIO (*beaming*).   The Government will pay twenty-five pounds to anyone holding open his house for travellers. The twenty-five pounds will buy – clothes. (THE GIRLS *gasp with joyful understanding*.) And the inn will bring – gentlemen.

(*Turning briskly to* AUNT LIZZIE.) A pedlar, did you say, Lizzie?

AUNT LIZZIE (*bewildered*). Yes. Clothes – turn this house into an *inn*! (*As* HORATIO *goes off.*) Your father! An ordained minister – I don't believe it!

SERAPHINA (*exultantly*). You will when the stage stops here next month.

ANGELINA (*marvelling*). Merchants from Halifax and Saint John –

SERAPHINA. Officers from the Army and Navy!

DULCINEA. All coming to *our* house!

AUNT LIZZIE (*alarmed*). I won't have it! You –

> (*Stops as* HORATIO *enters with* WILL KANE, *the pedlar, wearing a shabby green suit and snagged yellow hose, and with his dusty hat under his arm.* ANGELINA *glances at him and goes to sofa,* SERAPHINA *stares disdainfully, but* DULCINEA *gasps with pleasure and thereafter never takes her eyes off him.* KANE *is sober and businesslike, but addresses himself exclusively to* HORATIO, *ignoring the ladies and very uneasy when* DULCINEA *comes into his orbit.*)

> (ANGELINA *points at* DULCINEA *and giggles with* SERAPHINA.)

HORATIO. Now, my dears, here is a pedlar from Halifax with some excellent goods in his pack – isn't that right, my boy?

KANE. Yes, sir. Women's wear, mostly.

SERAPHINA (*jumping up eagerly*). Oh?

HORATIO. Let us see, then, what my daughter Angelina fancies – in a dress material.

> (*Pouting,* SERAPHINA *sits down again while* ANGELINA *comes forward.*)

KANE (*drawing forth samples*). This is very good calico, sir.

HORATIO (*seeing* ANGELINA's *disappointed look*). Something a trifle more elaborate, I think.

KANE (*showing a swatch of satin*). I don't know if this –

HORATIO. The very thing! I have always admired the colour of good claret. How does this suit you, Angelina?

ANGELINA (*fingering it*). It's beautiful!

SERAPHINA (*reaching in front of her*). That's *my* colour!

HORATIO (*gently pushing her back*). Well, Angelina?

ANGELINA (*nervously*). It's not *too* elaborate?

HORATIO. What do you think, young man?

KANE. It's what all the ladies wear in Halifax for evening parties.

HORATIO. Then it should do splendidly. Now we must have everything to go with it — bonnet, slippers, ribbons — and have you any flesh-coloured hose? (*Girls look the other way as* KANE *bashfully withdraws the hose and shows it to* HORATIO.) (*Briskly.*) Underthings. (*Reaction from women.*) Petticoats, shifts, chemises, garters — (KANE *draws them out for inspection one after the other.*) And one of those thingumabobs with stays. Excellent. I suppose they come in all sizes?

KANE. Oh, yes, sir.

HORATIO. Put them away, my boy — and I shall see you in Halifax when I go to see about the licence. Where will I find you?

> (DULCINEA *has jumped to help* KANE *put back the things and* KANE *is flustered — they struggle briefly over the corsets before getting them safely into the pack, then* DULCINEA *tenderly folds a pair of pantaloons, with adoring eyes on his embarrassed face, then they have a dodging match.*)

KANE. At the pantaloons — I mean — the red store at the — the lower end of — Granville! (*Escaping at last.*) Good day — and thank you! (*Exits kitchen.*)

> (DULCINEA *looks after him adoringly.*)

HORATIO (*with satisfaction*). There! We've made a good start. (*Sits down at table and begins to compose something on paper.*) Now — let me see —

ANGELINA (*going to* DULCINEA, *taking her firmly by the shoulders and turning her away from the kitchen.*) He's only a poor pedlar!

SERAPHINA. You can do better than that now, Dulcie!

AUNT LIZZIE (*rising and looking majestic*). About this inn-keeping notion, Horatio, I have been thinking it over. The idea is absolutely ridiculous – out of the question. (*As* HORATIO *pays no attention.*) Horatio! Horatio, what *are* you doing?

HORATIO. We must have a name for our inn. (*Reading.*) The Inn of the Wise Virgins. (*As all four women give shocked gasps.*) Well – perhaps somewhat obvious. (*Writes.*) The Three Maids Inn. How is that?

ALL THE GIRLS. Oh, yes, Papa!

AUNT LIZZIE (*desperately*). Horatio, I cannot permit you to –

> (*The girls surround her, joining hands in a circle and dancing round her.*)

DULCINEA. One for the money –

SERAPHINA. Two for the show –

ALL THE GIRLS. Three to get married and – (*pointing at* AUNT LIZZIE *laughingly*) four to go!

AUNT LIZZIE (*bursting furiously out of the ring*). We'll see – we'll see!

> (*The girls rush to* HORATIO *and hug him ecstatically.*)

FADE OUT.

MUSIC: *Bridge.*

FADE IN TO SAME SOME WEEKS LATER. *Afternoon. Fade in on* ANGELINA *arrayed in the claret gown, pirouetting before* DULCINEA *and* SERAPHINA.

DULCINEA (*peeking under the hem*). Lace on *every*thing!

SERAPHINA (*sulkily*). Papa must have spent a lot of that money.

ANGELINA (*smugly*).   The whole twenty-five pounds.

SERAPHINA.   What!

ANGELINA.   I tried to discourage him, but —

SERAPHINA (*outraged*).   That's a likely tale! You *pig*, Angelina!

ANGELINA (tossing her head).   Jealous cat!

> (*As they glare at each other,* AUNT LIZZIE *passes between them, goes to sofa and reverses cushions. The two girls return at once to their pugnacious poses.*)

AUNT LIZZIE.   Criminal extravagance!

ANGELINA.   Papa said only the best was good enough — (*preening herself*) for *me*!

SERAPHINA (*spitefully*).   Well, of course you *need* all the help you can get!

ANGELINA (*angrily*).   Thank you, Seraphina! You're always reminding me I'm the oldest, so it's only right —

SERAPHINA.   It's not right for you to have it all!

DULCINEA.   Shh!

> (HORATIO *enters briskly, with auger, and goes to wall on kitchen side.* SERAPHINA *rushes to him.*)

HORATIO.   Are you all ready? The coach should be here shortly.

SERAPHINA.   Papa, how could you!

HORATIO (*measuring the wall carefully*).   About here, I think.

SERAPHINA.   You've spent all the money on Angelina — what am *I* to wear?

HORATIO (*calmly*).   It really doesn't matter, my dear — no one will see you.

SERAPHINA.   Wha-a-a-t!

HORATIO.   You and Dulcinea will be in the kitchen doing the cooking. Angelina must not spoil her gown.

SERAPHINA (*wailing*).   That's not fair!

HORATIO. Oh, yes it is. Angelina is the oldest — she must be married first. You will each have your turn.

SERAPHINA (*bitterly*). When all the money's gone!

(AUNT LIZZIE *has been drawing closer and closer to* HORATIO *until she is alongside him. She puts her finger into the hole he has bored.*)

AUNT LIZZIE. What in heaven's name —

HORATIO. A mode of communication, Lizzie — a peep-hole to be exact. I must be able to afford assistance to my daughters when necessary.

AUNT LIZZIE. The Lord help us!

HORATIO. He will, if we do our part. Now, by means of the peep-hole, we may see and hear all that goes on, and thus support Angelina —

ANGELINA (*triumphantly*). And it will seem that I am doing the *cooking* as well!

DULCINEA. But isn't that rather deceitful?

HORATIO (*gravely considering*). Perhaps it might be called so, if our designs were worldly, Dulcinea — but (*his brow clearing*) in so moral a matter as matrimony, it is called — (*smile*) putting one's best foot forward.

DULCINEA. Oh, I see.

SERAPHINA (*explaining*). If women didn't put themselves in a good light, Dulcie, men might *miss* their virtues.

HORATIO. And then what would become of humanity? There is no point in doing a thing, unless you do it thoroughly.

DULCINEA (*nodding*). No half-measures.

HORATIO (*happily*). Precisely!

SOUND: *Coach arriving. Rattle of wheels, horses snorting, etc., driver shouting, 'Hold up, hold up there, whoa', etc.*

SERAPHINA. It's the coach!

ANGELINA. The coach!

DULCINEA.   The coach!

> (*All three girls run to hallway and look, one behind the other, with hands on hips of one in front, waggling their heads and rears as they try to see who is arriving.* HORATIO *comes up behind them.*)

HORATIO.   Each to your post now — it's time for action!

> (GREENGATE *enters.*)

GREENGATE.   Good   evening — Greengate,   farmer   from Cumberland.

HORATIO.   Good evening.

GREENGATE.   Supper as soon as possible.

HORATIO.   Mrs. Greengate?

GREENGATE.   No, I'm a widower.

SCENE II

OPEN ON KITCHEN. *Same time.*

> (HORATIO *is leading* OATES *in a confidential manner to the wall in which the peep-hole is bored. The girls scatter away from it as they see him come.*)
>
> (*As* OATES *nods and goes,* HORATIO *beckons to* ANGELINA.)

ANGELINA (*nervously*).   Well, Papa?

HORATIO.   A rich widower from Cumberland, one of those canny Yorkshire folk. A Mr. Greengate. Have a look, my dear. (ANGELINA *presses her eye to the hole.*) A well-preserved forty, I'd say. Blunt fellow — no nonsense about him. If he doesn't please you —

ANGELINA (*hastily*).   Oh, but he does! (*Primly.*) I mean — I think I prefer a mature gentleman, Papa!

HORATIO. · Very well. I shall help all I can. First — a good

dinner – then I shall see that you are left alone together. Keep
up a good fire – do a turn on the spinning-wheel perhaps – and
be sure to show him your hand-sewn quilts. Let *him* do most
of the talking. (ANGELINA *ticks off the instructions tensely on her
fingers.*) I have a parish call to make this evening, but I think
you will be all right for a few hours. I daresay we'll know –
(*smiling encouragingly*) one way or the other quite soon – he's
not the sort to waste much time courting!

CUT TO: AUNT LIZZIE *near by, listening, with compressed lips
and look of determination.*

DISSOLVE TO: AUNT LIZZIE'S *hands laying blankets in drawer
and closing it secretively.*

DISSOLVE TO: AUNT LIZZIE'S *hands pouring oil out of lamp.*

DISSOLVE TO: AUNT LIZZIE *pouring water over wood in fireplace and wood-box.*

DISSOLVE TO: *kitchen. Morning.*

(HORATIO *enters kitchen eagerly, but* DULCINEA *and*
SERAPHINA *look at him accusingly – washing up
breakfast dishes.*)

SERAPHINA. *Why* did you go *out* last night, Papa!

HORATIO. My duty –

DULCINEA. *Every*thing went wrong!

HORATIO. Dear me! What happened?

SERAPHINA. In the first place, Angelina's quilts disappeared.

DULCINEA. So she couldn't show them to Mr. Greengate.

SERAPHINA. We looked everywhere.

DULCINEA. Except in Aunt Lizzie's room – and *she* looked
there.

SERAPHINA. Then something went wrong with the spinning-
wheel.

DULCINEA. Poor Angelina couldn't spin two inches without
the thread breaking!

HORATIO. Dear me! Didn't I see Aunt Lizzie using it yesterday?

DULCINEA. Yes, and it was perfectly all right then! Next, the oil in the lamp gave out and they had to sit in the dark.

HORATIO (*startled*). In the dark!

SERAPHINA. Yes — and we couldn't see a thing! (*Pokes at peep-hole resentfully.*)

DULCINEA. Worst of all, there was no fire. The room was like ice!

SERAPHINA. The wood was soaking wet.

DULCINEA. As if someone had poured water over it.

HORATIO. Surely Angelina fetched dry logs from the woodshed?

ANGELINA (*enters with cup — pours coffee*). I couldn't, Papa. The woodshed door was locked, and the bolt stuck fast. (*But she does not seem upset, and smiles as she arranges flowers in a bowl.*)

HORATIO (*horrified*). My poor child. You had to sit there in the cold and the darkness all evening!

ANGELINA (*demurely*). It wasn't as cold as you might think, Papa. Have you ever heard of a custom in this country called — bundling?

HORATIO. Why, no — I can't say I have.

ANGELINA (*going with coffee*). It's very popular in New England, Mr. Greengate says!

CUT TO: *living-room. Same time.*

(ANGELINA *comes to table and sets down flowers gracefully.*)

ANGELINA. I hope your breakfast was satisfactory, Mr. Greengate.

GREENGATE. Aye — champion. (*He's nervous and uneasy; can't quite make up his mind.*)

ANGELINA. I'm glad. A hard-working man like yourself ought always to have hearty well-cooked meals set before him.

GREENGATE (*thoughtfully*). By gum, tha's right.

ANGELINA (*innocently*). I daresay it's difficult – on such a large acreage – to manage all the details of a household – alone.

GREENGATE (*heavily*). It is that.

ANGELINA (*sympathetically*). The loss of your good wife must be a great hardship to you.

GREENGATE (*loudly*). Miss Dogberry!

ANGELINA. Yes, Mr. Greengate?

GREENGATE (*frowning portentously*). Ah'm a plain-spoken man.

ANGELINA (*helpfully*). Yes?

GREENGATE. And when ah've owt to say, ah say it.

ANGELINA (*admiringly*). Yes, indeed.

GREENGATE. As ah tow'd tha last night, ah've important business in Boston and'll not be coomin' back this way again.

ANGELINA (*sadly*). Yes, I know.

GREENGATE. Tha said tha'd always wished to see Boston –

ANGELINA. I've longed for it!

GREENGATE. And, as tha just now said, Ah'm sorely in need of a wife. Wilt tha marry me and coom along?

ANGELINA (*rushing into his surprised arms*). Oh, sir – this is so sudden!

GREENGATE (*shyly attempting an embrace and then drawing back*). Ah don't dilly dally once ah've made up ma mind. Naturally, ah'll first speak with tha father – (*But* HORATIO *is already in the room, one hand behind his back.*)

HORATIO (*cheerfully*). Someone call?

MUSIC: *Sneak in special theme to announce impending wedding bells.*

GREENGATE (*startled*). Eeah! (*Slowly.*) Well, the fact is,

Reverend, ah've just now asked tha daughter to be ma wife and —

HORATIO (*quickly*). Permission granted! I wonder if you know how well you have chosen. (*Pats* ANGELINA's *arm fondly*.)

GREENGATE (*stammering a little*). Tha daughter'll s-suit me f-fine.

HORATIO. 'She looketh well to the ways of her household and eateth not the bread of idleness.' (*Looking at book in his hand in surprise*.) Why, what have we here? Offices of the Church! I say — we could have the ceremony now if you like.

GREENGATE (*dazedly*). But — we'll need a witness.

HORATIO (*projecting*). Tom! Seraphina. Dulcinea. Lizzie. (*They all troop in and line up before the astounded* GREENGATE *and* ANGELINA, *who is clingingly lovingly to his arm*.) My younger daughters — my sister-in-law — Tom, you must be best man.

OATES (*grinning*). Gotta hand it to you, mister — you court quick.

GREENGATE (*weakly*). When once Ah mak up ma mind, nowt stands in ma way.

ANGELINA (*adoringly*). I do love a determined man.

>   (GREENGATE *beams at this and puts a manly arm round her.* HORATIO *pushes the sulky* AUNT LIZZIE *into place and opens his book*.)

HORATIO. Dearly beloved — we are gathered together —

FADE OUT WITH MUSIC: *Triumphant wedding bells.*

FADE IN TO SAME, A SHORT TIME LATER. *Morning.* DULCINEA *and* SERAPHINA *are waving good-bye at the window.*

SOUND: *Coach fading off in the distance.*

DULCINEA (*singing happily*). Wasn't papa wonderful?

AUNT LIZZIE (*entering with scowl*). Shameless – utterly shameless.

HORATIO (*entering with something over his arm*). Lizzie, do *you* happen to know what bundling means?

AUNT LIZZIE (*crossing to sofa and reversing cushions*). I certainly do! It's a most immoral custom in parts of this new country for courting couples to share a blanket in order – (*her eyes fix on the tumbled blanket lying over the end of the sofa*) in order to keep warm – (*she touches it, is suddenly horrified*) in a cold room! (*She sinks down on sofa, defeated.*)

HORATIO (*slightly shocked*). Dear me! However, you've helped two people to find each other.

SERAPHINA. Papa – it's my turn now – and there's no money left to buy me – (*Gasps as* HORATIO *holds out the claret gown.*) Papa!

HORATIO. Mr. Greengate will be buying Angelina's gowns from now on.

SERAPHINA (*holding it up to herself delightedly*). Of course – and then – after I'm married, it can be altered for Dulcinea.

DULCINEA. Oh, no. It's lovely – but a man must love *me* for *myself.*

SERAPHINA. Silly! You're not still dreaming of that poor pedlar? Why, he couldn't keep you in calico!

AUNT LIZZIE (*sniffing*). Dulcie is independent – like me. I've been happier without a man.

SERAPHINA (*wickedly*). How do you *know*, Aunt?

AUNT LIZZIE (*folding blanket angrily*). I know one thing. There'll be no more of this ridiculous matchmaking. *I* shall see to that!

FADE OUT ON APPLE-TREE THROUGH WINDOW.

FADE IN TO APPLE-TREE WITH AUTUMN LEAVES FALLING. PAN OVER SIGN 'THE TWO MAIDS INN'.

DISSOLVE TO: *kitchen. Afternoon.*

(AUNT LIZZIE *is knitting,* DULCINEA *busy with some cooking,* SERAPHINA *is staring sulkily out of the window.*)

AUNT LIZZIE (*smiling sourly*).   The coach isn't due again till Friday!

DULCINEA.   Three *months,* Seraphina! You'll *have* to choose someone *soon!*

SERAPHINA (*sulkily*).   There hasn't been anyone in the *least* suitable so far!

CUT TO: *exterior rectory. Same time.*

(LIEUTENANT HONEYWELL, *brushing dust from hat and shoulders, comes up to sign, looks at it, gazes around impatiently, smacks whip against his hand.*)

HONEYWELL.   Service here! Boots!

CUT TO: *interior rectory (living-room). Same time.*

(HORATIO *seated, reading or writing, looks up in surprise, listens.*)

HONEYWELL (*off*).   Confound it!

(HORATIO *rises and looks towards door as* HONEYWELL *enters.*)

HONEYWELL.   Where is everyone in this — (*Sees* HORATIO.) This *is* an inn?

HORATIO.   Oh, yes, certainly! Where did *you* come from?

HONEYWELL.   From Annapolis —

CUT TO: *kitchen. Same time.*

(*The girls are all listening near the peep-hole.*)

HONEYWELL (*off.*)   Honeywell's the name — Lieutenant — Her Majesty's Navy.

(SERAPHINA *pushes the others aside and looks through peep-hole.*)

SERAPHINA (*joyfully*). Oh, Dulcie!

DULCINEA (*eagerly*). Well?

SERAPHINA. Oh, *yes*! He's just the sort I've *always* wanted!

AUNT LIZZIE (*stamping her foot*). Ohhh! Fiddle!

CUT TO: *living-room. Same time.*

HORATIO (*still bewildered*). But the coach wasn't due today –

HONEYWELL (*impatiently*). Travelling horseback – which reminds me – I want my beast seen to. He went lame a mile back.

CUT TO: *kitchen. Same time.*

SERAPHINA. Oh, my hair – the claret gown – (*She dashes away.*)

DULCINEA. Well, thank goodness – we've got someone for Seraphina at last.

AUNT LIZZIE (*scowling*). Don't be too sure. She hasn't caught him yet!

CUT TO: *living-room. Same time.*

HORATIO (*hospitably*). Sit down, sit down, my dear Lieutenant – you must be tired. I shall see to your horse presently.

HONEYWELL (*sitting down and looking around discontentedly*). I suppose I'm becalmed in this foul backwater until my horse is fit to ride.

HORATIO (*genially*). Never mind. (*Pushing tobacco jar forward as* HONEYWELL *takes out pipe.*) We are quite used to taking care of gentlemen. So you're a naval officer. An interesting life – the sea.

HONEYWELL (*wearily*). I like it.

HORATIO.   Healthy life. Carefree. (*Sits down and takes out his own pipe.*)

HONEYWELL.   As free as the birds.

HORATIO (*suggestively*).   Unless one has home ties?

HONEYWELL.   In that respect, I am fortunate.

HORATIO.   No ties?

HONEYWELL.   None.

HORATIO (*beaming*). Ahhh! (*Lights pipe.*) Matrimony steadies a chap.

HONEYWELL.   Too true! Brings him to a standstill.

HORATIO (*with mild reproof*).   My boy, marriage is a state ordained by God not only for His purpose, but for the happiness of man.

HONEYWELL.   No doubt. Still, it ties a chap down.

HORATIO.   A good ship needs an anchor.

HONEYWELL (*smugly*).   Not often, if she's fast.

HORATIO (*dismayed*).   So you're not attracted to the fair sex.

HONEYWELL (*with something approaching animation*).   On the contrary! I am one of its most fervent admirers.

HORATIO (*relieved*).   Then, my dear boy, all you need is the love of a good woman.

HONEYWELL (*languidly*).   By all means — so long as she doesn't insist on matrimony. (*Raising an eyebrow at* HORATIO.) And believe me, I'm up to all their tricks.

(HORATIO *looks disturbed.*)

SERAPHINA (*demurely*).   You called me, Papa?

HORATIO (*jumping up in surprise*). Eh? (*Takes in the picture of* SERAPHINA, *demure and smiling in the claret gown, and his face clears.*) Oh, why, yes — yes *indeed*! Lieutenant, may I present my daughter. Seraphina — Lieutenant Honeywell.

(HONEYWELL's *languid and disdainful manner drops from him suddenly as he rises with a surprised and appreciative look at* SERAPHINA.)

HONEYWELL (*bowing low*). Your servant, mistress.

SERAPHINA (*curtsying*). Yours, sir. May I ask if you intend to remain a few days?

> (*He crooks his arm and* SERAPHINA *takes it, they walk to sofa and* SERAPHINA *seats herself gracefully, while the* LIEUTENANT *leans over her in obvious admiration.* HORATIO *has hastened to pour a glass of wine from decanter.*)

HONEYWELL. Yes. My leave isn't over yet. And I find the air in this place — stimulating.

HORATIO. A glass of wine, Lieutenant?

HONEYWELL (*absently reaching back and taking it without removing his gaze from* SERAPHINA). Thank you. It is rather a surprise to find a lady so charming and fashionable in this out-of-the-way place.

SERAPHINA. I expect you have a wide acquaintance amongst the ladies.

HONEYWELL. I cannot recollect one at the moment. You have driven them all out of my head.

SERAPHINA. I fear they would not thank me for that.

> (HORATIO *looks at them benignly and starts to move softly out of the room, but he meets* AUNT LIZZIE *coming in.* AUNT LIZZIE *marches straight to the sofa, brushing the* LIEUTENANT *aside, and sits down beside* SERAPHINA — *blocking the* LIEUTENANT's *view of her.*)

AUNT LIZZIE (*calmly*). How cool it is these fall afternoons — just the sort of weather to sit indoors by the fire — and engage in conversation.

CUT TO: HORATIO *and* DULCINEA *in kitchen at peep-hole. Fade out on their dismayed faces.*

FADE IN TO: *living-room. Evening.*

> (SERAPHINA *enters quickly. After a hasty look around,*

she sits on sofa, and waits expectantly. After a
moment, HONEYWELL *appears, looks around ner-*
vously, then smiles and hastens to SERAPHINA.)

HONEYWELL.   Miss Seraphina! Alone – at last!

(But as he goes to seat himself beside her, we hear
AUNT LIZZIE'S *loud cough.* HONEYWELL *is caught in*
mid-air. He straightens with a grimace and bows to
AUNT LIZZIE *as she enters.)*

AUNT LIZZIE.   Good evening! *(She sits beside* SERAPHINA.)

SERAPHINA *(smouldering).*   Did you come down to look for
something, Aunt?

AUNT LIZZIE.   Why, no.

SERAPHINA.   You are generally abed and asleep at this hour!

AUNT LIZZIE *(gaily).*   I'm not at all sleepy this evening. I
think I would enjoy a nice chat.

SERAPHINA.   We were just saying – we didn't feel like chat-
ting this evening – weren't we, Lieutenant Honeywell.

HONEYWELL.   Oh – er – yes, certainly.

AUNT LIZZIE *(calmly).*   Then – we'll – just – sit.

(She squeezes up close to SERAPHINA, *indicating the*
other side to HONEYWELL. *He squeezes in, scowling,*
tries to signal behind her head to SERAPHINA, *but*
AUNT LIZZIE *keeps her head in the way. She knits*
placidly.)

CUT TO: *kitchen. Same time.*

DULCINEA *(turning away from peep-hole to her father).* Three
days, and they've hardly had a moment alone! And he *leaves*
tomorrow!

HORATIO *(worried).*   I have spoken to her several times.
(Reaches out and picks up poker, looks at it solemnly.) I fear
the time has come for more direct action.

DULCINEA *(horrified).*   Papa!

CUT TO: *living-room. Same time.*

> (AUNT LIZZIE *deliberately drops her ball of wool, and it rolls out into centre of room. She looks at it.* HONEYWELL *looks at it. They look at each other, wooden-faced, and finally he gets up reluctantly, walks slowly to the ball, looks at her again, bends swiftly, and picks it up. She holds out her hand demandingly as he reaches her. He slaps it into her hand, turns furiously, and strides across to another chair and sits down.* HORATIO *appears.*)

HORATIO (*gently*). Lizzie.

AUNT LIZZIE (*gaily*). Good evening, Horatio.

> (*She doesn't look up and anyway* HORATIO *has the poker behind his back.*)

AUNT LIZZIE. Sit down — you won't disturb us.

HORATIO (*louder*). Lizzie —

AUNT LIZZIE. As I was just saying to Seraphina and the Lieutenant —

HORATIO (*in an awful tone*). Lizzie!

AUNT LIZZIE (*looking up startled*). What —

HORATIO (*pointing towards the kitchen with poker*). Kitchen.

AUNT LIZZIE (*indignantly*). Horatio, if you think — (*Weaker.*) Horatio?

HORATIO (*looking solemnly at the poker*). 'David prevailed over the Philistines with a sling shot and with a stone!'

AUNT LIZZIE (*gasping and running*). Mercy!

> (HORATIO *lays the poker down gently by the fireplace, yawns, nods politely to the two on the sofa, and goes quietly out.*)

Scene III

FADE IN ON INTERIOR RECTORY (*living-room*). *Same time as last act.*

> (HONEYWELL *is staring after the retreating back of* HORATIO, *bewildered, but* SERAPHINA *is smiling.*)

HONEYWELL (*wonderingly*).　Have they really gone?

SERAPHINA.　Oh, yes.

HONEYWELL (*realizing*).　Then – then, at last – we really are alone! Seraphina!

SERAPHINA (*primly*).　Please – I have not given you leave to be familiar.

HONEYWELL (*puzzled*).　Familiar?

SERAPHINA.　You called me Seraphina. That is a privilege I reserve for old friends and – (*shyly*) some day, of course, my husband.

HONEYWELL (*sitting back quickly*).　I beg your pardon, Miss Dogberry!

SERAPHINA.　Perhaps in time I may come to look on *you* as an old friend.

HONEYWELL (*gloomily*).　Hardly likely. I'm off to Halifax in the morning.

> (*He sits glumly with his face turned away until he hears a delicate sniff. He turns in amazement.*)

HONEYWELL.　You're crying! Seraphina! Then you do care!

SERAPHINA (*sniffing some more*).　No, no –

HONEYWELL.　But you do, darling, you do! (*Clasping her triumphantly.*) We were meant for each other! (*As she looks up meltingly, he adds hastily.*) Meant to be friends, that is. (*She turns away.*) It was fate. From the moment I saw you – so lovely – so charming –

SERAPHINA. Please, sir, don't speak so. You will turn my poor foolish head. (*She jumps up from sofa.*)

HONEYWELL (*trying to turn her chin*). If only I could.

SERAPHINA (*eluding him*). I am only an innocent country girl, unaccustomed to pretty speeches.

HONEYWELL (*pursuing her*). I will accustom you, dearest girl – surely you're not afraid of me?

SERAPHINA (*helplessly*). I am so alone – and unprotected.

CUT BRIEFLY TO: *kitchen side of peep-hole where* DULCINEA *is stuffing her hanky in her mouth to keep from laughing out loud.* HORATIO *beside her puts a warning finger to his lips.*

HONEYWELL. Let *me* be your protector – your knight – your dear friend! (*He's all over her now, and he backs her down on to sofa.*)

SERAPHINA (*collapsing in his arms*). I must go now.

HONEYWELL (*caressing her arm*). Soon. Not now.

SERAPHINA (*faintly*). Yes, now – at once.

HONEYWELL (*gathering her in his arms*). Don't leave me.

SERAPHINA (*struggling faintly*). I must. It's very late.

HONEYWELL. Not too late –

SERAPHINA (*relaxing completely*). I really *must* go now.

(*He kisses her with practised passion. As they embrace*, SERAPHINA *waggles her fingers over his shoulder and we see* HORATIO *standing behind the sofa.*)

HONEYWELL (*exultantly*). Mine, all mine.

SERAPHINA (*shyly*). Then you do love me – truly?

HONEYWELL (*recklessly*). Love you? I adore you! I shall always adore you!

(*He goes to kiss her again. A loud cough from* HORATIO *and he freezes, then leaps to his feet, horrified.*)

HONEYWELL. The devil!

SERAPHINA (*smiling sweetly*).   No — only Papa.

HORATIO (*sadly*).   So I must lose yet another child.

HONEYWELL.   What!

HORATIO (*going to him gravely with his hand held out*).   I ought to hate you, sir, but I too was young once. (*Shakes limp hand.*) You have my blessing.

HONEYWELL.   Blessing!

HORATIO (*whipping out his little book*).   More than my blessing! I shall perform the ceremony here and now!

HONEYWELL.   Ceremony!

HORATIO.   So that your happiness may not be delayed.

HONEYWELL (*turning to* SERAPHINA, *panic-stricken*).   Seraphina —

SERAPHINA (*casting herself lovingly into his lax arms*).   Darling — of *course* I'll marry you!

HONEYWELL (*groan*).   Caught! Must face it, I suppose — other men have. (*Miserably.*) Daresay I'd have come to it in time. (*Takes a breath, comes stiffly to attention*). Very well, sir — aim true — and fire!

HORATIO (*calls*).   Dulcinea — Lizzie. (*They slip into the room.*) (*Finding the place in the book.*) Dearly beloved — (*Notices* HONEYWELL *is on the wrong side of* SERAPHINA. *This will never do. He gently moves the numbed* HONEYWELL *from* SERAPHINA's *left to her right, and steps back.*) Dearly beloved, we are gathered together —

FADE OUT TO:
MUSIC: *wedding bells, segue to bride.*
FADE IN TO: *apple-tree covered with snow.*
DISSOLVE TO: *interior rectory (living-room).   Morning.*

(HORATIO *is peering out of the window.* DULCINEA *is reading by the fire,* AUNT LIZZIE *knitting as usual.*)

HORATIO (*sighing*).   No coach today, I fear. (*Goes to peep-*

hole and wipes it with his finger.) Dust. Soon the roads will be impassable with spring mud. My dear, finding a bridegroom for you may be difficult.

AUNT LIZZIE. That won't worry Dulcinea. *She* doesn't *want* a bridegroom.

DULCINEA. I want to stay with you, Papa.

HORATIO. Most flattering, my dear, but we'll see — you may change your mind.

AUNT LIZZIE. No. Dulcinea takes after me. (*Dulcinea looks a bit worried at this.*) Sensible. I intend to leave her *all* my money — so she can have an independent life like mine.

HORATIO. My dear, why are you so averse to marrying?

DULCINEA. I'm not — averse, exactly.

HORATIO. But you refuse to wear the claret gown.

DULCINEA (*earnestly*). Papa, I don't want a man just because he's a *man* — not just any traveller who happens along.

HORATIO. No, no.

DULCINEA. I want a man I can love — a man who was *meant* for me.

HORATIO (*vigorously*). Certainly!

DULCINEA. So I must wait for the right one.

AUNT LIZZIE (*sourly*). Many a woman's said that and she's *still* waiting.

HORATIO. But — dear me — how are we to know this true lover when he comes along?

DULCINEA (*dreamily*). *I* shall know. (*Getting up and swaying across the room.*) He'll be handsome, and rather shy. I shall only need to look into his eyes and — as he takes my hand, I'll just say (*dropping a curtsy towards the door*) Sir, I am so happy you have come.

> (*As she drops her head at the bottom of the curtsy, the door opens and* WILL KANE *stands there.* DULCINEA *sits down with a bump.*)

KANE (*confused*). I didn't know I was expected.

(*He holds out his hand to* DULCINEA *and helps her up, and apparently forgets to let go of it. They stare at each other all through the following.*)

HORATIO (*pleased*). Hullo – where did you spring from?

KANE (*still looking at* DULCINEA). Will Kane – of Halifax – I'm travelling horseback.

HORATIO. Oh – so that's it.

AUNT LIZZIE (*accusingly*). Why – you're the pedlar!

HORATIO. Of course! You remember, Dulcinea – last spring?

DULCINEA (*breathlessly*). I remember.

HORATIO (*meaningly*). You had better see to dinner, my love.

DULCINEA. Yes, Papa. (*She goes off, still looking over her shoulder at* KANE, *and he watches her out of sight.*)

AUNT LIZZIE (*jumping up to* KANE *angrily*). What are you doing here? What do you mean – coming here dressed like a gentleman – what are you up to?

HORATIO (*shocked*). Lizzie!

AUNT LIZZIE. Last spring he came pretending to be a poor pedlar. Now he turns up, dressed fine enough to turn any girl's head. Horatio, send him away!

HORATIO. My dear Lizzie –

KANE. I can explain, sir. My father owns the store I work for. Last spring he sent me out peddling, to gain experience. Now I am on my way to take charge of his branch store in Saint John. I've only stopped for a bite to eat.

AUNT LIZZIE (*calming down at once*). Oh. You're not *staying*. (*Exiting.*) That's different!

HORATIO (*to himself dreamily*). Farmer – naval officer – merchant!

KANE. Pardon?

HORATIO. Eh? Oh, nothing – nothing at all. (*Bustling to pour out glass of wine from decanter on table.*) A glass of Madeira?

KANE. Thank you. I suppose my horse will be cared for? I left her in the stable.

HORATIO. Oh, I shall see to her. And my daughter will see to *you*. (KANE *pauses with the glass half-way to his lips, and* HORATIO *adds hastily.*) That is — to your dinner. You must not dream of going on today — there's a storm coming.

KANE. I'm afraid I'll have to, sir. I must catch the boat at Annapolis.

HORATIO. We'll see, we'll see. Excuse me now — I must find out what Dulcinea is planning — that is, preparing! Make yourself at home, my boy —

CUT TO: *kitchen. Same time.*

(AUNT LIZZIE *is poking about the cupboard, scowling.*)
AUNT LIZZIE. Dulcinea, where did you — (*Looks around and cannot find* DULCINEA.) (*Projecting.*) Dulcinea?

HORATIO (*bustling up*). Where's Dulcinea?

AUNT LIZZIE (*resentfully*). I don't know, and I don't intend to do all the work. (*Taking off her apron.*) You can do the cooking for a change. (*Throws apron at him.*) I've got a headache! I'm going to lie down. (*Marches off.*)

HORATIO. Lizzie — wait! Oh, bless my soul — (*Begins to tie on apron back to front.*) At such a time! Oh, there you are. (*As* DULCINEA *appears.*) — The first thing — (*Double take as he sees she is wearing the claret gown.*) My dear, it suits you best of all.

DULCINEA. Thank you, Papa. (*Uneasily.*) Nothing's prepared. Where's Aunt Lizzie?

HORATIO (*switching apron round to the front*). Aunt Lizzie is unwell, but I shall manage. Do your best — I like the looks of that young man. Go and amuse him until the meal is ready.

DULCINEA (*suddenly scared*). Amuse him! How? Oh, Papa, I'm frightened. What shall I say?

HORATIO.   Why, Dulcie, I've never known *you* with nothing to say!

DULCINEA.   But this is different. This is *important*! I shall be wondering all the time what he is thinking of me.

HORATIO (*firmly*).   Just what you must not do! The best way to overcome self-consciousness is to think of the other person. Forget your*self.*

DULCINEA (*feverishly nodding*).   Forget myself!

HORATIO.   Draw him out — ask him questions.

DULCINEA (*ticking them off on her fingers*).   Draw him out — ask questions.

HORATIO.   Let *him* do most of the talking.

DULCINEA.   Let *him* do the talking. (HORATIO *nods.*) Well, I'll try. (*Goes off muttering.*) Ask questions — ask questions —

CUT TO: *living-room. Same time.*

> (KANE *is standing with his glass of wine. As he sees* DULCINEA, *he hastily drinks it off. They eye each other nervously.*)

DULCINEA.   Good — afternoon.

KANE (*with a stiff bow*).   Afternoon.

DULCINEA.   Mr. Kane?

KANE (*nodding jerkily*).   From Halifax.

DULCINEA.   I'm — (*Pause.*) Did — did you have a nice ride?

KANE (*sitting down stiffly beside her*).   Not very. (*Blurting.*) Have you lived long in these parts.

DULCINEA.   Oh, yes — since — (*Pause.*) (*Remembers.*) (*Primly.*) How were the roads?

KANE.   Bad. (*Pause.*) Is — is this good farm country?

DULCINEA (*hurriedly*).   Do *you* have a farm?

KANE (*Pause*).   No.

DULCINEA (*vexed with herself*).   Oh, of course not! You're in business.

KANE (*fast*).   Is your father's parish large?

DULCINEA.   Not very. (*Pause.*) Is business good in Halifax?

KANE.   Are you —

DULCINEA (*at the same time*).   Do you skate?

KANE (*confused*).   Sorry. What?

DULCINEA.   Skate!

KANE.   No. (*He looks around desperately for something to talk about.*) I — I —

DULCINEA (*breaking into a headlong speech she can't control. She should say as much of it as possible before he stops her*).   I love to skate — do they skate in the city — I mean, do they go skating — or is it sleigh-riding they do — I hear it's quite popular — I understand the militia has a bobsled club — do they really coast down the Citadel — have you any family, Mr. Kane — brothers, I mean, or sisters — are you fond of them? Are they married — or living at home? What part of Halifax do you live in — they say — (KANE *can't stand it any longer, seizes her in desperation and kisses her, then looks horrified.*) (*Breathing hard and all smiles and blushes.*) Goodness!

KANE (*aghast*).   I'm sorry!

DULCINEA.   That's all right. (*Comes down into room again.*)

KANE.   I didn't mean to.

DULCINEA (*disappointed*).   You didn't?

KANE.   I had to stop you asking questions.

DULCINEA (*crushed*).   Oh! I see. (*Turns her back.*)

KANE.   You kept on and on.

DULCINEA.   But so did you.

KANE.   You wouldn't stop.

DULCINEA.   Neither would you. (*Suddenly they look at each other — and burst out laughing.*) (*Marvelling.*) Why — you were as nervous as I.

KANE (*amazed*).   You're shy too!

DULCINEA.   Weren't we silly.

KANE (*sheepishly*).   I don't know how to talk to a girl. Never been able to get started. Someone told me a good way was to ask questions.

DULCINEA (*laughing*).   It must work — you're talking to *me* now.

KANE.   So I am!

DULCINEA.   Do sit down, Mr. Kane.

KANE (*sitting down beside her happily*).   Certainly. Funny, I'm not nervous any more. Feel as though we were a couple of chaps talking — I mean — as though we'd been acquainted a long time.

DULCINEA (*smiling*).   We have been — ever since last spring. Tell me — *do* you like skating?

KANE.   Yes, but I'm not very good.

DULCINEA.   I could teach you.

KANE.   Would you? Wonderful!

(HORATIO *enters with tray and sets food on table*.)

HORATIO.   Tea is ready in the other room. Not fancy — but filling.

(KANE *leads* DULCINEA *to the table and sits down opposite*.)

DULCINEA.   I can do spirals and inside circles.

KANE.   I've never had much time for fun — for skating, and so on.

DULCINEA (*happily*).   I'll take you out to the pond first thing in the morning.

KANE.   Great! And then we could — (*Pause*.) (*Face falls*.) Oh, lord, I forgot. I won't be here tomorrow.

DULCINEA.   Won't be here?

KANE.   I must go on as soon as I've eaten, or I shan't reach Annapolis in time for the boat.

DULCINEA (*stricken*).   Couldn't you go tomorrow?

KANE.   There isn't another sailing for a week. If I'd known, I might have left Halifax a day sooner — or even a week sooner!

DULCINEA.   Couldn't you take a later boat?

KANE (*brightens, then glum again*). I couldn't tell my father I'd missed the boat to go skating.

DULCINEA (*sadly*). Couldn't you?

CUT BRIEFLY TO: HORATIO *at kitchen side of peep-hole, listening, and looking worried.*

KANE (*wryly*). You don't know my father. He'd never understand my taking a vacation along the way for no reason — I mean, no *good* reason — that is, a reason *he* could understand.

DULCINEA. I see.

(HORATIO *crosses quietly in back and out front door.*)

KANE (*mournfully.*) It can't be helped.

DULCINEA (*hopefully*). The next time — (*As he shakes his head, dismayed.*) You mean you won't be coming this way again?

KANE. Dad says a chap ought to keep his nose to the grindstone, like he did, not go gallivanting about the country. (*As* DULCINEA's *head drops.*) I'm awfully sorry. I'd certainly *like* to skate with you. We seem to — get along.

DULCINEA (*mournfully*). What good is it, when we won't see each other again. Doesn't your father want you to ever get married?

KANE (*startled*). Married!

DULCINEA (*hastily*). I mean — if he keeps you at work all the time, how are you to meet any — any young ladies — socially?

KANE. I never thought of that. You'd need time to court a young woman.

DULCINEA. Not *much* time. I know a couple who were wed after only one meeting — the very next day in fact.

KANE (*disapprovingly*). That's a bit short in my opinion. A chap needs to know a girl — three or four days at least.

DULCINEA (*sadly*). I used to think that, too.

(*They look at each other for a moment, sadly, then*

KANE *looks at the clock, turns back, looks again with double take of alarm.*)

KANE.   Good lord — it's later than I thought!

(*He jumps up and starts to hurry into his coat.*)

DULCINEA (*holding up his cup*).   Your tea!

KANE.   No time. Sorry.

DULCINEA (*almost in tears but determined to retain her pride*). Well, I mustn't keep you, Mr. Kane, if you really must go. (*Holding out her hand.*) It's been most p-pleasant m-me-et-ing you.

KANE.   I suppose, if I ever do come back, you'll have forgotten all about me. (DULCINEA *shakes her head.*) You might even be — married.

DULCINEA (*turning away with a sob*).   I don't think so!

KANE.   Well — (*Starts towards the door.*) (*Turns back.*) Good-bye, Dulcinea. (*She can't speak.*)

(*He turns away.*)

SOUND: *Sudden yells from outside. Loud frightened whinnies of horse, galloping hoofs, fading off.*

DULCINEA (*lifting her face from her hands*).   Oh, what is it?

HORATIO (*off*).   Help! Help!

KANE.   My horse!

DULCINEA.   My father!

(*They both rush off and a moment later come back supporting* HORATIO *between them. He is all over mud, his clothes are mussed, and he's limping.*)

KANE.   What happened, sir?

HORATIO (*groaning*).   The mare — oh, my leg!

DULCINEA.   Oh, poor Papa — are you hurt?

HORATIO.   It's my leg — that is, my arm — it hurts — (*They help him on sofa.*)

KANE (*putting* HORATIO's *feet up on sofa*).   Is it broken? Let me see —

HORATIO (*holding up arm pathetically dangling*). See — quite useless.

AUNT LIZZIE (*rushing in*). Mercy! What's happened?

HORATIO. Mr. Kane's horse — reared — bowled me over — and bolted.

KANE. *Bolted?* (*Dismayed.*) Gone?

HORATIO (*weakly*). Something must have frightened her.

AUNT LIZZIE. Wolves! I told you I saw one lurking near the barn yesterday. Blankets! (*Rushes off.*)

KANE. My poor mare!

HORATIO (*reassuringly*). She was running very fast the last I saw of her. Some neighbour will pick her up. The trouble is (*eyeing* KANE *sideways*) it won't be known at first where she came from. (*As* KANE *looks puzzled,* HORATIO *has a new spasm and groans again.*)

DULCINEA (*anxiously*). Oh, Papa dear, don't try to talk.

HORATIO. But I'm thinking of poor Mr. Kane. He has no means of leaving here — perhaps for days.

DULCINEA. Oh!

KANE (*realizing*). Not for *days*?

HORATIO. You'll miss your boat. Most unfortunate. Whatever will you do?

KANE (*starting to smile*). There's nothing I *can* do. (*To* DULCINEA.) Is there? (*She shakes her head, smiling widely.*) (KANE *turns to* HORATIO *and tries to look solemn.*) I'm sure my father will understand. After all — an accident — (*He reaches out for* DULCINEA's *hand.*)

AUNT LIZZIE (*rushing in with blanket*). Oh, never mind all the talk. Off to the kitchen — heat water — bring bandages!

DULCINEA (*happily*). Yes, Aunt Lizzie.

KANE (*smiling*). Certainly, Aunt Lizzie.

> (*They pass their joined hands over* HORATIO's *head and go off.*)

MUSIC: *Sneak in wedding bells, faint but triumphant.*

AUNT LIZZIE (*fussing*). Here — let me fix that pillow —

HORATIO. No, No! (*Rearing back and toppling off sofa, catching himself on his 'useless' arm.*)

AUNT LIZZIE (*staring at his arm*). Your arm! (*Suspiciously.*) Useless?

HORATIO (*picking himself up off floor hastily*). Ah — perhaps it isn't broken.

AUNT LIZZIE. Perhaps it isn't! And perhaps that mare *didn't* knock you over! (*Voice rising.*) Horatio — did you drive that animal away on purpose?

HORATIO (*nervously*). I say, Lizzie, don't shout.

AUNT LIZZIE (*triumphantly*). So you *do* have something to hide. And *this* time you *admit* you were deceitful!

HORATIO. Well — possibly — just a little. (*Happily.*) But I don't see how my little ruse could possibly hurt anyone — and it does mean the happiness of two young people. (*Beaming.*) I really think Kane will be my favourite son-in-law.

AUNT LIZZIE (*aghast*). You mean — already?

HORATIO. Before the week is out, depend on it. My worries are at an end.

AUNT LIZZIE (*collapsing in chair*). And mine are just beginning!

HORATIO. Come now, Lizzie. You can set up a home in Halifax and be quite comfortable. It's fortunate you have the means.

AUNT LIZZIE. But I haven't!

HORATIO. Eh?

AUNT LIZZIE (*tragically*). I lied. I have no money.

HORATIO (*indignantly*). What? None at all?

AUNT LIZZIE (*dismally*). Only enough to bury me.

HORATIO. And all this time you led us to believe —

AUNT LIZZIE (*spiritedly*). I had to! I couldn't be an object of charity! (*Slumping.*) Oh, what shall I do now — homeless, penniless, friendless —

HORATIO (*firmly*).   Not friendless, Lizzie. You know *I* shall do anything I can —

AUNT LIZZIE (*angrily*).   I should think you would! It's all your fault!

HORATIO.   *My* fault?

AUNT LIZZIE.   Yes! If you hadn't married them off, I'd be safe here — and comfortable. The very least you could do — (*Pause.*) (*Slowly with dawning excitement.*) Yes, the very *least* you could do — claret suits me too — see!

> (DULCINEA *has entered with basin,* KANE *following with handful of bandages. Now* AUNT LIZZIE *darts to her, lifts up skirt of dress and holds it a little in front of her hopefully.*

HORATIO (*collapsing on the sofa*).   Oh, no — oh, no — oh, no!

CURTAIN